PUGS, PUG DOGS, AND THE PUG
Your Perfect Pug Book

PUGS, PUG DOGS, PUG PUPPIES, PUG BREEDERS, PUG CARE, PUG FOOD, PUG HEALTH, PUG TRAINING, PUG BEHAVIOR, BREEDING, GROOMING, HISTORY AND MORE!

By Matthew Masterson

© DYM Worldwide Publishers, 2020.

I0088973

Published by DYM Worldwide Publishers 2020.

ISBN: 978-1-913154-18-9

Copyright © DYM Worldwide Publishers, 2020
2 Lansdowne Row, Number 240 London W1J 6HL

ALL RIGHTS RESERVED. This book contains material protected under
International & Federal Copyright Laws & Treaties. Any unauthorized
reprint or use of this material is strictly prohibited. No part of this book
may be reproduced or transmitted in any form or by any means, electronic,
mechanical, or otherwise, including photocopying or recording, or by
any information storage or retrieval system without the express written
permission from the author.

Copyright and Trademarks. This publication is Copyright 2020 by DYM Worldwide Publishers. All products, publications, software, and services mentioned and recommended in this publication are protected by trademarks. In such an instance, all trademarks & copyright belonging to the respective owners.

All rights reserved. No part of this book may be reproduced or transferred in any form or by any means, graphic, electronic, or mechanical, including but not limited to photocopying, recording, taping, scanning, or by any information storage retrieval system, without the written permission of the author. Pictures used in this book are royalty-free pictures purchased from stock photo websites with full rights for use within this work.

Disclaimer and Legal Notice. This product is not legal or medical advice and should not be interpreted in that manner. You need to do your own due diligence to determine if the content of this product is right for you. The author, publisher, distributors, and or/affiliates of this product are not liable for any damages or losses associated with the content in this product. While every attempt has been made to verify the information shared in this publication, neither the author, publisher, distributors, and/or affiliates assume any responsibility for errors, omissions, or contrary interpretation of the subject matter herein. Any perceived slights to any specific person(s) or organization(s) are purely unintentional. We have no control over the nature, content, and availability of the websites listed in this book.

The inclusion of any website links does not necessarily imply a recommendation or endorse the views expressed within them. DYM Worldwide Publishers takes no responsibility for, and will not be liable for, the websites being temporarily or being removed from the Internet. The accuracy and completeness of the information provided herein and opinions stated herein are not guaranteed or warranted to produce any particular results, and the advice or strategies contained herein may not be suitable for every individual. The author, publisher, distributors, and/or affiliates shall not be liable for any loss incurred as a consequence of the use and application, directly or indirectly, of any information presented in this work. This publication is designed to provide information regarding the subject matter covered. The information included in this book has been compiled to give an overview of the topics covered. The information contained in this book has been compiled to provide an overview of the subject. It is not intended as medical advice and should not be construed as such. For a firm diagnosis of any medical conditions, you should consult a doctor or veterinarian (as related to animal health). The writer, publisher, distributors, and/or affiliates of this work are not responsible for any damages or negative consequences following any of the treatments or methods highlighted in this book.

Website links are for informational purposes only and should not be seen as a personal endorsement; the same applies to any products or services mentioned in this work. The reader should also be aware that although the web links included were correct at the time of writing, they may become out of date in the future. Any pricing or currency exchange rate information was accurate at the time of writing but may become out of date in the future. The Author, Publisher, distributors, and/or affiliates assume no responsibility for pricing and currency exchange rates mentioned within this work.

Table of Contents

CHAPTER 1

Introducing the Pug

The Pug is often called the comedian of the dog world. With its fun-loving personality and lovable, wrinkly face, it's easy to see why it's one of the most popular breeds in the United States and around the world. They've held a consistent spot in the top 20 of the AKC's ranking of most popular breeds and were #4 in the UK Kennel Club rankings for 2018.

The cute Pug dog can be the ideal pet for many families.

Adorable Pugs pack a lot of personality into a small package. They're very intelligent, extremely loyal, and don't take up a lot of space. The fact that they're also easy to groom and don't have high exercise needs makes them the perfect pet for apartment living and other urban environments.

Unlike many breeds of dog, the Pug was bred purely to be a companion. This is one of the reasons they're typically affectionate and loyal. While they can be stubborn and headstrong, the laid-back Pug gets along just as well with other animals as it does with people, making it an ideal family pet.

Of course, even cute Pug puppies aren't the right fit for everyone. Pugs are long-lived dogs, with lifespans of 15 years or more, making them a long-term commitment. You want to make sure you're ready for Pug ownership before you jump in—and this Pug book is here to help! Consider it your Pug 101 Primer that will teach you how to find and buy a Pug, the best supplies for the breed, as well as how to groom them, train them, and keep them healthy. You'll also learn the history of the breed and get the basic scoop on next level Pug owner questions, like how to show and breed them.

The crazy Pug can bring you years of love and entertainment. Let's get started on your journey to becoming a new Pug parent!

CHAPTER 2
Pug History

The original Pug breed is believed to date back to as many as 2,400 years ago. Since then, they've enjoyed a long and storied history, starting in the Far East and spreading all over the world.

Though there's evidence of an old Pug breed dating back centuries, formalized breeding practices weren't started until the 19th century—well after the Pug had been introduced to Europe, and largely had the same appearance as Pugs today. Nonetheless, we can determine most of the Pug's history through anecdotal evidence, as well as its depictions in art from both China and Europe.

The long history of the Pug dates back to ancient China.

Ancient Origins

The ancient Pug looked a bit different than the breed we know and love today. The old Pug breed was first developed in Asia. Pug looking dogs can be seen in art from Tibetan monasteries, as well as the imperial courts of both China and Japan. This ancient Chinese Pug was known as Lo-Sze or a Foo dog. The original Pug look had a Pekingese-like build, though with the shorter coat and smooth tail typical to Pugs.

What Was the Ancient Pug Bred For?

Most modern dogs—even those kept primarily as pets today—were originally bred for a more practical function, such as a guard dog or a hunting aid. Not so with the Pug. From its earliest iteration, cute Pugs were bred solely as pets and companions.

They would provide entertainment at Imperial courts, serving as lapdogs and foot warmers for the Chinese and Japanese nobility.

Chinese Pug to English Pug

When trade routes opened between China and Europe, Pugs were one of the most popular new imports. Dutch and Portuguese traders were the first ones to bring these dogs to the west, beginning the breed's association with the Netherlands.

Pugs served much the same function in European courts as they had in those of the East: lapdogs, jesters, flea catchers, and foot warmers. In the 1570s, the Pug became the official dog of the House of Orange after Prince William's pet Pug Pompey woke him during an invasion by the Spanish, allowing him to escape.

It was through the House of Orange the Pug made its way to England. After the marriage of Mary II to William II of Orange, the Pug gained popularity throughout the British Isles. Queen Victoria was a Pug fan, as well, not only breeding them herself but also helping to found Britain's Kennel Club in 1873.

The English Pug received another surge of popularity in the mid-19th century. After the British sacking of China's Imperial Palace in Beijing, British soldiers brought back several Pugs—including black Pugs, previously unseen in the west. The breed's appearance changed in other ways, as well. The Pug of the late 19th century had a smaller stature and flatter face than its predecessors.

How Did the Pug Get its Name?

No one really knows the full answer to this question. In fact, the name "Pug" wasn't associated with the breed until the late

18th century. When they were first brought to Europe, Pugs were often referred to as Dutch mastiffs or dwarf mastiffs, due to their sturdy bodies and wrinkly faces. In Germany and the Netherlands, they were sometimes known as Mopshonds (or Mops for short). This comes from the Dutch word "to grumble," given because of their frowning expressions.

There are several theories about the origin of the Pug name. A 19th century author, J.H. Walsh, believed it was from the Latin *pugnus*, meaning fist, which the Pug's profile was said to resemble.

The name might have also derived from the 17th and 18th century European habit of keeping marmoset monkeys. These wrinkly-faced primates were popular pets and often were referred to as Pugs. Whatever its origins, the name Pug was standardized by the time formal breeding programs began in Europe.

The Pug Comes to America

Pugs didn't instantly catch on in the United States, and they were introduced much later than other breeds. The first Pugs made it to America after the Civil War. Despite its late introduction, Pugs were accepted as a breed in the AKC in 1885, in the first batch of breeds added after the club's 1878 founding. This meant they were accepted alongside popular breeds like the Beagle, Dachshund, and Greyhound.

The American Pug nearly vanished in the early 20th century. There were only 15 Pugs registered with the AKC in 1926. There were a few dedicated breeders, however, mostly along the East Coast. Together, they formed the Pug Dog Club of America in 1931, keeping the breed alive in the United States.

By the mid-'40s, there were over 150 Pugs registered with the AKC or the PDCA. The breed's popularity continued to grow through the '50s and '60s. By 1955, they were 20th in popularity, and they rose to 17th by 1965. They've been consistently among the most popular breeds in the nation ever since.

Famous Pugs

Since they first became a breed, Pugs have been known to grace the homes of the rich and famous: the imperial family of China, the nobility of Europe, and even present-day celebrities. Among the famous people who have owned Pugs are Jenna Elfman, Paula Abdul, Charlie Sheen, and Billy Joel.

Funny Pugs are also a favorite breed of the silver screen. There was a Pug in the 1986 film *Adventures of Milo and Otis*, and one famously played an alien in 1997's *Men in Black*. The 2018 film *Patrick Pug* depicts a spoiled Pug willed to a young woman by her grandmother. Other films featuring Pugs include *Runaway Bride, Pocahontas,* and *Dune.*

Pugs make great candidates for internet stardom, too. There are plenty of Pug memes out there, many of which involve Guppy the Pug, whose social media accounts have more followers than most people.

CHAPTER 3

Understanding the Pug

L ike Bulldogs and Shar-Pei, Pug wrinkles are the breed's main defining feature. The addition of the button or rose ears and the round, bright eyes make up the Pug dog breed's facial profile. And its face in many ways matches its personality, giving it a happy or crazed expression that suits the breed's often clownish behavior.

Pugs offer up a lot of surprises. They're sturdier than most dogs in the toy group—and they have a different disposition, too. You're more likely to hear them snoring or snuffling than yipping like a Yorkie, and they tend to be laid-back rather than high-strung. These factors are why many Pug owners describe them as a big dog in a small body.

Before seeking out a Pug dog for sale, take the time to learn what the breed is all about.

The AKC Pug Standard

Even if you don't plan to show your Pug, looking at the AKC Pug standard is the best way to know what you can expect from the breed physically. In terms of body shape, the Pug is square and muscular. It has straight legs, balanced between the front and back, and of a moderate length for its height.

While the Pug's coat can come in a few colors (more on that in a bit), it's generally tight to the body, with a smooth, soft texture. A hard or wooly texture suggests the influence of another breed somewhere in the Pug's lineage.

The Pug muzzle is short and square with a slight underbite. The round head is topped by small ears, that can have two different shapes. A button ear is when the ear flap-folds forward over the insides and is the preferred shape for showing. Some Pugs have rose ears, where the top flap folds back and reveals the inner ear. The Pug's comical expression mostly comes from its eyes, which are dark and round, and often seem to be smiling. This expression is considered crucial to the breed in the show ring.

How Big Does an Adult Pug Get?

On average, Pugs usually weigh around 14-18 pounds (6-8 kilograms) and stand 10-13 inches tall (25-36 centimeters). While they can get larger, the AKC standard specifies they be no more than 20 pounds (9 kilograms) and stand no more than 15 inches tall (38 centimeters).

A big Pug isn't uncommon. The biggest Pug in the world weighs over 46 pounds (21 kilograms). A giant Pug like this is unusual, but a large Pug can weigh upwards of the AKC weight limit and still be healthy.

Identifying the smallest Pug in the world is a bit trickier due to the presence of the teacup Pug. This tiny Pug is either a purebred with the dwarfism gene or a crossbreed with another toy breed (often a Chihuahua). These miniature Pugs can weigh as little as 3 pounds (1.4 kilograms) when full-grown.

Temperament and Personality

The first thing you often hear about Pugs is how much they love to play and have fun. While there are different types of Pugs and each dog is an individual, the majority of them are upbeat, spunky, and outgoing, and can seem like puppies even once they're full-grown.

You might expect such a playful dog to have high energy, but in this sense, the Pug has a bit of a split personality. Most adult Pugs are perfectly content with a mostly sedentary lifestyle. While others are more active, they're usually not as high-energy as most breeds in their weight class.

Pugs are generally very outgoing dogs. Shyness is rare in a well-socialized Pug, and while they're loyal to their owners, they're rarely territorial or aggressive. It's rare to see a Pug snap except in self-defense. Mostly they just want to be around people and are happy to meet strangers—one reason they don't function well as guard dogs.

How long do Pugs live?

Like many smaller dogs, Pugs are long-lived as a breed. The longest living Pug was named Snookie. He died in 2018 at the age of 27. While your family pet might not set a record for the oldest Pug, many live 15 years or more. Pugs also stay younger longer than other breeds. Many remain agile and mobile even after age 7, the age at which most dogs are considered to be seniors.

Coat Colors

The AKC only recognizes two coat colors for the Pug: Fawn and black. Other kennel clubs, including the CKC and the UK Kennel Club, also recognize silver and apricot as acceptable types of Pugs. Other colorations do exist, though they are rare and considered as faults (for reasons we'll get into below).

The Fawn Pug

The fawn Pug is the most common coat color, accounting for almost 2/3rds of registered dogs. You might also see them referred to as a tan Pug or a black and tan Pug. These dogs have an undercoat of light brown or tan over most of their body, with black markings around the face, ears, and down the center of the back. A fawn Pug puppy may not fully have these markings, but they always develop by adulthood.

The Black Pug

Approximately 1/3rd of all registered Pugs are black, making it the second most common coat color. Finding black Pugs for sale shouldn't be difficult. Some owners think of a black Pug as almost a different breed from other coat colors. Though there's no scientific reason the black Pug dog should behave differently; however, anecdotally, this does seem to be the case. They tend to be a bit more stubborn and assertive, which can be challenging when it comes to training.

This baby black Pug is already a comedian.

One physical difference with black Pugs is that they don't always have two coat layers. This may mean they shed less than their lighter-furred counterparts, though this won't be the case with every black Pug. In terms of shade, the fur can have a blue-black appearance (preferred in competition) or a rusty black hue that's closer to a very dark brown.

The Apricot Pug

Next in rarity is the apricot Pug, which makes up about 4% of registered dogs. Like fawn Pugs, they have a paler body with a black mask, which might not show up right away on apricot Pug puppies. They differ from fawn Pugs in that there's an orange undertone to the body's coat.

The Silver Pug

The silver Pug is the rarest of the accepted coat colors. It is a pale gray color, often referred to as a warm stone. It is also the lightest of the acceptable coat colorations, in some cases looking nearly white. If there is a touch of brown or tan in the coat, it is called a silver fawn Pug. Like apricot and fawn Pugs, a silver Pug must have black facial markings.

The Merle Pug

The term "merle" refers to a pied coat or one that is patterned over the entire body in patches. A merle Pug usually has patches of blue or blue-gray over fawn or silver, which gives it the alternate name blue Merle pug. This may be accompanied by blue eyes or multi-colored eyes. True merle Pugs are very rare. You'll likely have to search a while to find a merle Pug for sale. In many cases, this aberrant coat is the result of another breed's influence in the dog's line. This is why merle Pugs aren't accepted in kennel club competitions.

Albino Pugs

Albinism is possible in Pugs, as it is in most breeds, although it is exceedingly rare and considered a fault in the show ring. An albino Pug will not only have a pure white coat with no mask or markings, but it will also likely have pink eyes, due to its inability to produce melanin. Albino Pugs may have more health concerns than other coat colors, as well.

Other Pug Colors

You may see other colors of the Pug out there and wonder why these coats aren't accepted by the AKC. Generally, it's the same as the reason for the merle Pug's exclusion: the aberrant coat most often indicates the presence of another breed's genes somewhere in the dog's lineage.

It should be noted this is only an issue if you plan to show your Pug. If you're looking for a family pet, it doesn't matter whether you buy a grey Pug, an all-white Pug, or a red Pug. They will be just as affectionate, and may even have fewer health concerns thanks to their more diverse genetic background.

That being said, other potential coat colors for the Pug include:

- **Blonde Pug.** Also called a golden Pug, these have a coat that's similar to apricot or fawn, but without the facial markings.

- **Brindle Pug.** Similar to merle, brindle is a pattern of light and dark colors. With a Pug, the dominant colors are typically black and gray. A brindle Pug puppy may lose one of the colors as it ages and have a more silver or gray coat as an adult. Finding a true brindle Pug for sale can be tricky.

- **Chinchilla Pug.** Another rare color, these gray Pugs, lack darker markings and remain a silvery hue all over their entire lives.

- **Chocolate Pug.** Also called a Brown Pug, this is a very rare color. These Pugs are brown from head to toe, with no darker facial markings.

- **Platinum Pug.** This coat happens when one of the parents is a white Pug or carries the recessive white coat gene. They may have black or white markings on their face and ears, with a gray or white color over the rest of the body.

- **White Pug.** These dogs are all white, and may or may not have facial markings. They're differentiated from albinos by the pigment in their eyes.

CHAPTER 4

Pugs as Pets

S ome breeds started out as hunters and evolved into family companions over time, but Pug-looking dogs have been family pets throughout their history. The modern Pug is true to this history. That's the reason it's one of the most popular breeds worldwide, year after year.

No breed is the perfect pet for everyone, though. Like with all purebreds, Pugs have specific care requirements that you'll want to make sure you can handle before you bring one home. Before you start searching for "Pug puppies for sale near me" in your browser, let's go through what Pugs are like as pets.

The playful Pug can be a perfect companion for humans of all ages.

Pros and Cons of Owning a Pug

Pugs make great pets because...

- **They can live anywhere.** The Pug's small stature means it doesn't need a lot of space to be happy. This makes them great city dogs since they can live in any size apartment comfortably.

- **They don't act their size.** Lots of people think of small dogs as yippy and excitable—and for most small breeds, this is true. However, Pugs don't exhibit these typical small dog traits. Their barking tendencies and temperament are more similar to those of medium-sized breeds than they are to Chihuahuas or Terriers.

- **They're low-maintenance.** Grooming a Pug is easy (as you'll see later in the book). They also don't have very high exercise requirements—your average Pug dog is more interested in cuddling than running.
- **They make friends with everyone.** Pugs aren't picky about how they share their affection. kids, cats, other dogs—if they're wanting to play, so is the Pug. While every dog is different, as a breed, Pugs are friendly and outgoing.

The challenges of owning a Pug include…

- **They can be messy.** Even though the Pug has a short coat, they still shed. They are also known chewers and will get into anything they can reach, including garbage cans, laundry baskets, and other potential things they can make a mess out of.
- **They don't like being alone.** Pugs are a social breed. They'll give you a lot of love—and they need an equal amount of love in return. Many adult Pugs are laid-back enough to tolerate being left alone during the day, but some will suffer from separation anxiety, even if well-trained and socialized.
- **They don't deal well with heat.** Pug wrinkles are more likely to develop bacteria and other infections in a hot environment. They're also prone to overheating. If you live in a hot climate, Pugs may not be the best dog for you.
- **They're noisy (day and night).** Pug barking isn't a huge concern, but they make other noises—including snoring, which is notably loud. This is largely due to their flattened faces (which cause other health issues we'll discuss in chapter 13), so it's not something you can easily correct. Keep this in mind if you're looking for a dog to sleep in bed with you.

How much do Pugs shed?

The Pug's close coat is deceptive. They have a lot more hair than you probably realize, and it's relatively long—it just grows horizontally, along the Pug's body, instead of sticking up vertically.

Like many breeds, most Pugs actually have two coats. The topcoat is the long, straight hair you see. Underneath this is a soft, fluffy layer. The exception to this is some black Pugs, who only have one coat. If you want a Pug but are bothered by shedding hair, a cute black Pug might be the one you want.

How loud is the snoring of a Pug?

Pug snoring is normal. While you'll find plenty of tips from Pug owners about lessening or preventing it, it's often just a trait of the breed. A snoring Pug can be just as loud (or louder) than a snoring human. If you're sensitive to noise at night, you'll want to train your Pug to sleep in its crate when it's a puppy to avoid having your sleep interrupted.

Pugs and Kids

The Pug is a natural companion for kids. Since they're small, they're unlikely to knock kids over or hurt them. Their muscular build, meanwhile, means they're sturdy enough to avoid injury, and they're also unlikely to bite or nip, even during rough play.

While Pugs and kids get along well, children under the age of 5 should be supervised any time they're interacting with the dog, for the safety of both. Kids in grade school and older can normally handle and even take care of a Pug themselves.

Pugs and Other Animals

Pugs get along famously with other Pugs. Keeping two Pugs isn't much more difficult than one, and they can keep each other company if you work during the day. While Pugs often get along with other breeds of dogs, as well, they do prefer to be the Alpha of their pet pack. They'll often end up the de-facto leader, even if your other animals are bigger or older. If your Pug is headstrong during training, he's likely to be a bit bossy with canine companions. Keep this in mind if you're introducing your Pug to another dominant dog, especially a larger dog that could injure him.

Most Pugs get along famously with other animals, too, including cats. Some Pugs do have a chase instinct, though this is rare in indoor Pugs. Others can be a bit too friendly with felines, though they also learn quickly—most will figure out they should give kitty some space after they get clawed once or twice. Still, you should supervise the initial interactions between Pugs and cats closely. Chapter 9 has some tips on socializing Pugs with cats and other dogs if you have them in your home.

In many cases, Pugs and cats can be best friends.

Space and Environmental Needs

As we said above, Pugs don't need a lot of space—but they do need the right space. Make sure it's not too hot in the Pug's main environment. Overheating can lead to breathing and heart trouble, especially in the long-term.

The small stature of the Pug may necessitate some adjustments to your home, as well. Adult Pugs can safely navigate most staircases, though tile and wood can lead to slips and falls.

What Does Owning a Pug Cost?

How much a Pug puppy costs depends on where you get it (something we'll delve into in Chapters 5 and 6). As far as long-term costs, however, Pugs are a relatively inexpensive breed. While they do love food, their small size means they don't eat much. They're also relatively healthy and don't often need expensive health care.

The long-term costs of owning any dog vary considerably. What kind of food you buy, how quickly your dog goes through toys, how many vet visits he needs a year—these will all affect the cost. As a general rule, you should expect to spend between $500 and $1,000 (£375-£775) per year.

CHAPTER 5

Pug Breeders

Since the Pug is such a popular breed, you shouldn't have any difficulty finding Pug puppies for sale, and you won't typically have to wait to get a puppy, as is often the case with rarer breeds. Unfortunately, this same popularity means there are some Pug breeders that care more about profit than the health of their animals. Avoiding disreputable breeders is the most important first step in finding healthy baby Pugs for sale.

A real Pug puppy can be expensive, but they're well worth the investment.

There are a lot of ways you can find a breeder and make sure they're on the up-and-up. Doing your research and knowing which questions to ask is the best way to find the best Pug for your family.

There are a few advantages to buying a Pug from a breeder, as opposed to adoption or rescue. The biggest one is that you'll know the puppy's pedigree, which is a breeder term for their lineage. This means you can be sure it's a real Pug and is necessary if you plan to show your animal. Even if you're looking for a family pet, knowing the pedigree is helpful in predicting and avoiding hereditary diseases.

Breeders are also excellent sources of information for new Pug owners. They will know about the best local vets and trainers and can put you in contact with Pug clubs or other Pug fanciers. Most reputable breeders are happy to serve as a resource throughout the dog's life, as well.

Finding Pug Puppies For Sale

Finding cute Pugs for sale used to mean scouring the newspaper classifieds or checking your local phone book. Today the internet is most people's first stop when they're shopping for baby Pug puppies. Many breeders have websites where they'll post pictures of their breeding animals and any Pug puppies currently for sale. While this is no substitute for visiting the kennel in person, it is very helpful in identifying which breeders you want to contact, especially if you're looking for a specific coat color.

You can find a list of breeders in the Bonus Chapter at the back of this book. Typing "Pug puppies for sale near me" in your internet browser will bring up even more options. Keep in mind that any breeder can set up a website for their kennel, so you can't assume every breeder on the internet will have healthy Pug puppies.

Kennel clubs and Pug clubs also maintain searchable lists of breeders. They will typically only list breeders who are registered with the club and have a reputation for following good breeding practices. These clubs also organize dog shows and other events where you can meet a variety of Pug breeders (and their dogs) in one place. While they typically won't have puppies for sale at the show, you can get their contact information and watch how they interact with their animals. Check the calendar of local Pug clubs to find out when they're hosting their next Pugfest or Pug show.

Identifying a Reputable Breeder

First and foremost, you want to find a breeder whose main concern is the health of their animals. Steer clear of any breeder who seems anxious to get rid of their animals, or tries to pressure you into a purchase. A good breeder will have as many questions for you as you have for them. The interaction should feel like a two-way interview, with both of you working toward the same goal: making sure you take home the right Pug for you, not just the first Pug that comes along.

Second in importance is ensuring the breeder is knowledgeable—not just about breeding dogs in general, but Pugs in particular. They should be able to answer any questions you have about caring for your Pug and to do so with authority.

So, how do you make sure a breeder is on the up and up? The answer is two-fold: by asking the right questions, and by paying attention during your visit to the kennel.

Questions you should ask:

- **How long have you bred Pugs?** The longer a breeder has worked with Pugs, the more familiar they'll be with the specific needs of the breed—and this usually translates to healthier, happier puppies.

- **What health certifications can you show for your puppies?** There should be documentation of vet visits for check-ups and vaccinations. In addition, most breeders will have their animals certified to be clear of eye problems through the Canine Eye Registry Foundation (CERF) and should have proof of testing for other hereditary conditions.

- **Are there any health problems in the puppy's line?** Many hereditary health issues don't become apparent until the Pug is full-grown. The life-long health of previous Pugs in the lineage is the best way to predict these diseases in puppies.

- **How often do you produce litters?** A female Pug should not breed every time she's in heat. Over-breeding tells you the breeder is either poorly educated or profit-oriented—either way, that breeder is someone to avoid.

- **At what age do your dogs begin to breed?** Pugs should not start breeding before the age of 2. Breeders who start them earlier are again either focused on profits or uneducated on proper breeding practices.

- **What is the goal of your breeding program?** Some kennels focus on breeding championship show dogs. Others are focused primarily on improving the health of the Pug breed or breeding family pets. None of these are wrong answers as long as the breeder does have a goal for their program.

- **What is your policy on returns?** Ideally, your relationship with your Pug puppy will be for life. A good breeder should be prepared for any contingency, however, and would rather take the Pug back than have it abandoned if you can't care for it in the future. A strict no return policy is a warning sign of a profit-oriented breeder.

- **Do the parents or puppy have any faults?** This is mainly a concern if you plan to show your Pug. If you're more in the market for a family pet, a puppy with superficial faults may be a more affordable option, since in most cases, these won't impact the animal's temperament or health.

What should you look for at the kennel?

Paying a visit to the kennel is an important step in any new puppy purchase. The Pug's popularity means you should never be forced to buy a puppy sight-unseen, and it's unlikely you'll need to travel far to find a reputable breeder.

The first thing you should evaluate is the cleanliness of the kennel. There should be no offensive odors or visible pests and insects. While some messiness can be expected with puppies, including spilled food or recent accidents, you should be able to tell that the puppies' pen was cleaned recently. Look over the area to make sure the food and water are plentiful and clean, as well, and that there are sufficient toys and other comforts available to the puppies.

You should also make a point of visiting with the Pug's parents if the option exists. Some breeders may only keep females and pair them through a stud system, in which case the father may not be available to meet. If the breeder declines to let you meet the mother for the sake of the animal (e.g., she had a recent litter and isn't ready yet for visitors), this isn't a warning sign. If they refuse for other reasons, though, or if they don't keep the mother on-site, this is a red flag.

Finally, watch the puppies themselves. Happy puppies will be active, friendly, and playful. Watch the breeder interact with the puppies, and be wary if they seem fearful, aggressive, or resistant to handling.

Black Pug puppies for sale have the widest price variation of any of the coat colors.

How Much Does a Pug Puppy Cost?

A purebred Pug costs between $450-$1,500 per puppy on average (£350-£1,150). Having said that, a purebred Pug price can go as high as $6,000 or more (£4,675) if its lineage is exceptional. There are several factors that influence the price of a Pug puppy, including the pedigree of the puppy and the size, location, and reputation of the kennel. A Pug puppy whose parents are Best in Breed champions will cost more than one from parents untested in the show ring.

One significant factor in the average Pug puppy cost is the rarity of the coat color. This means you'll usually spend more on average for black Pug puppies or white Pug puppies than fawn Pug puppies. You'll see the difference looking at the average cost of different coats below:

- Apricot pug puppies: $650-$1,300 (£500-£1,000)
- Fawn Pug cost: $500-$1,500 (£400-£1,150)
- Black Pug price: $900-$3,500 (£700-£2,700)
- Brindle Pug puppy cost: $3,500 + (£2,700+)
- White Pug price: $1,800-$2,500 (£1,400-£2,000)
- Silver Pugs for sale price: $1,200-$3,500 (£950-£2,700)

The price of apricot and silver Pugs especially will vary depending on location and is typically higher in the UK, Europe, and Canada, where these coats are considered acceptable for competition.

CHAPTER 6

Pug Adoption and Rescue

One unfortunate side-effect of the Pug's popularity is that it's more likely to show up in rescue shelters than many other purebreds. The good news is the even-tempered Pug rarely has trouble bonding with a new family. An adopted Pug will be just as adorable, loving, and crazy as one you buy from a breeder.

If you're looking for cheap Pugs, adoption can be a great way to go. There are some things to be aware of before you start searching out Pug puppies for adoption, however. Many Pugs are put up for adoption by loving owners who have experienced a life change, like a big move or a new baby. In other cases, the animals are rescued from neglectful or even abusive environments, and that can have a lasting effect on the Pug's physical and mental health.

Just like with buying from breeders, the key is to do your research and know what you're getting into. If you're considering adopting a Pug, this chapter will help you figure out where to look, what to look for, and whether a rescue animal is a good choice for you.

The baby Pug price can be a lot lower if you can find one up for adoption.

Pros and Cons

The advantages of adopting a Pug are…

- **It can help to lower the cost of your Pug dog.** As you saw in the last chapter, the purebred Pug price can be pretty steep. Rescue organizations do have an adoption fee, but it's significantly less than what you'd pay at a breeder. Most Pugs for adoption have already been vaccinated and sterilized, saving you that future expense.

- **Rescued Pugs may be trained and socialized.** A Pug up for adoption has already lived with other people, and may already be used to other animals. Sometimes they'll even already be housebroken and know basic commands, especially if you find adult Pugs for sale.

- **You'll still get a lot of years with your Pug.** Pugs are hearty and have a long life-span. Even if you adopt a Pug who's a few years old, you can still enjoy a decade or more of companionship.

- **You'll be helping a homeless Pug.** Bringing home any Pug is a treat, but there's a special joy that comes with giving a good home to a Pug that doesn't have one.

The disadvantages of Pug adoption include…

- **You won't get to be picky.** You're unlikely to find baby Pugs for adoption. It's also rare to find specialized coat colors or teacup Pugs for adoption in most instances. If you're particular about how your Pug looks, adoption may not be for you.

- **There may be a waiting list.** There are lots of people who want Pugs but can't afford a puppy from a breeder. Unlike a breeder, the availability of Pugs for adoption is random, and sometimes the demand outpaces the supply.

- **Adopted Pugs may not be suitable for showing or breeding.** If you're looking at the rescue page on a Pug breed club, the listed animals may come with pedigrees. This isn't a guarantee, however. Rescues may also be spayed or neutered, which makes them ineligible for conformation (and obviously, for breeding).

- **You don't always know the Pug's full history.** A lack of pedigree means you don't know the health history of the Pug's line, making it harder to predict hereditary diseases. You also don't always know how the Pug was treated and cared for by its previous owners, which can lead to unexpected health problems or personality quirks down the line.

How Do I Find Pugs for Adoption Near Me?

First, your best opportunity is to check with Pug clubs and Pug-specific rescue organizations. The Pug Dog Club of America and Pug Club of Canada each have a rescue component on their website, where they help members re-home their pets and find homes for abandoned Pugs. You can find information for both groups, as well as a number of regional Pug rescue groups, in the Bonus Chapter at the back of this book.

The local Humane Society or animal shelter is another place you can check. Any purebred is relatively rare in these kinds of shelters, but you may be able to sign up for notifications when a Pug arrives. You'll expand your options if you're willing to adopt a mixed Pug, which can also make an excellent pet (more on that in Chapter 18). Rescue shelters provide basic health care for all their animals, treating any ailments they came in with and will make you aware of any continuing health concerns. They also spay and neuter all their animals.

There's always the dream you'll find baby Pugs for free advertised in the newspaper. You can still check the classifieds, but internet marketplaces have largely taken over. Websites like http://www.adoptapet.com and http://www.petfinder.com let you narrow your search to a specific breed. They can be a way to find cheap Pugs for sale, especially if you're willing to travel. The disadvantage of these sites is that they're unvetted. Sellers fill out basic information about their animals, but there's no guarantee of the Pug's health until you've brought him home to your vet.

Pug puppies for adoption

Finding Pug puppies for sale through an adoption website or breed rescue organization is pretty rare. Similarly, most of the dogs that turn up in shelters are 6 months or older. If you specifically want a puppy and don't want to go through a breeder, you'll need to put in a lot of leg-work. Ask local shelters if nearby breeders ever turn in un-sold animals. You can also set alerts on the sites mentioned above for Pugs in a specific age category. Even with all this effort, you may be waiting a while.

Finding trained Pugs for sale

If you're specifically looking for a well-behaved adult Pug, you may want to consider buying a retired breeding or show dog. While many breeders keep their retired Pugs as pets, some sell them to good homes so they can focus on their next generation.

A show-trained Pug for sale is likely to be more expensive than your average rescue. Still, it will be lower than the breeder's Pug puppy cost. There's also the advantage of knowing the dog has been impeccably cared for and is free of genetic health problems if it spent time in the show ring or was part of a reputable breeding program.

A trained adult Pug can be a lot easier to care for than a puppy— and they'll love you just the same.

What Does Adopting a Pug Cost?

As we mentioned above, the initial cost is low—usually somewhere around $100-$200 (£75-£150). Some shelters will also give you a discount for a second dog, making it an especially economical option if you're looking to adopt two Pugs.

One thing to keep in mind is that rescues may come with additional expenses. You'll pay more in vet costs if they have health issues. If you adopt an untrained adult Pug, a trainer can be another hidden expense—Pugs are notoriously stubborn, and this can make them difficult to train when they're full-grown.

Where Not To Buy a Pug

There is an unfortunate dark side to the puppy sale industry. Large commercial breeders, known colloquially as "puppy mills," keep their animals in inhumane environments, using unsafe and harmful breeding practices that are focused on making a profit rather than producing healthy, happy animals. Unfortunately, the popularity and small size of the Pug make it a frequent victim of these immoral companies.

Many of these puppy mills sell their animals to large pet stores. Because of this, you should avoid buying any Pug dog breeds you find in pet stores, especially rare coats, teacup Pugs, and Chinese Pugs for sale. Pet stores also keep their animals in small enclosures, where they're given inadequate human interaction. A puppy from a breeder is more likely to be healthy and well-socialized.

It can be tempting to "rescue" animals from a pet store, but you should resist this temptation. Spending money on a puppy mill Pug only gives more profit to these unsavory practices. If you want to rescue an animal, the methods listed above are a much better way to do so.

CHAPTER 7

Choosing a Pug

Whether you get your Pug from a breeder or a shelter, the key to a lasting, happy relationship is to find the right dog for you. It can often be very difficult to say no to cute baby Pugs, but you should do your best to look past the wrinkles and pay attention to warning signs that they may not be the best pet.

There are a few other decisions you'll have to make, as well, including how many dogs you want and whether a female Pug or male Pug. This chapter will take you through all the important questions you should ask yourself before you decide which Pug to bring home.

Searching for "Pugs near me" is just the first step in getting your new pet.

Identifying Healthy Pug Puppies

A healthy Pug puppy should be alert, energetic, and friendly. They might be shy the first time you meet them at the breeder, but they should adjust quickly and come to investigate you. Shyness, suspiciousness, or aggression could be signs of an improperly-socialized puppy—and remember, your future companion's mental health is just as important as its physical well-being.

Watch the puppy move around. They should be able to walk easily, without limping or listing to the side. Listen to how the puppy breathes, too. Respiratory issues are relatively common in Pugs, so keep an ear out for rattling or rasping, which are signs of a problem.

You can learn a lot about a puppy's health by looking at his face. Look inside his mouth to make sure the teeth are white and the gums nicely pink. Check that the eyes are bright and wide—squinting, watery eyes or discharge from the eyes could indicate an infection or genetic issue. Make sure the nose isn't running, either, and that there's no odor or discharge from the ears.

Finally, feel and evaluate the Pug's coat as you pet him. It should be bright and a consistent length all-over. A dull coat or bald patches likely point to a parasite infestation or other health issues.

Male Pug vs. Female Pug

Both male and female Pugs can make great companions. If the dogs are fixed (e.g., spayed or neutered), there is little difference between the genders when it comes to health. An unspayed female will go into heat twice a year. A dog in heat exhibits both physical and emotional symptoms, including a greater desire to escape. An un-neutered male, on the other hand, will be more likely to have accidents inside, even after he's housebroken.

The stereotype is that males are calmer and more cuddly but also more difficult to housebreak. Females are considered to be both smarter and more independent, which can also translate to stubbornness or aloofness. In truth, though, each dog is different, and there's no solid evidence male and female Pugs act differently.

Puppies vs. Adult Pugs

Many people instantly assume they want a puppy, but there can be advantages to getting an adult Pug, as well. With an adult, what you see is what you get. Since the Pug is full-grown, you'll be able to see most hereditary health issues, which may not be apparent in a puppy. The dog's adult coat will have come in, too, and you'll know if there are any physical faults that would disqualify it from the show ring.

In most cases, an adult Pug will also be easier to care for. Raising a Pug puppy is a lot of work. You can think of it like having an active toddler in the house. They'll need constant supervision until they're trained and socialized, and they make a lot more messes, including accidents or destroying personal possessions by chewing.

With an adult, you might not have to do as much work, either. In many cases, they'll already be housebroken and have basic obedience training. At the very least, they're usually already socialized and familiar with following daily routines. It's also likely they've already been spayed or neutered and have received their vaccinations. With a pug Puppy, you're starting from scratch. You'll be responsible for socializing and training, as well as the initial veterinary care. The flip side of this is that adults are tougher to train if training is required.

The big advantage of getting a Puppy is that you'll be in control of how it's brought up. You'll be better able to mold it into your perfect dog, rather than working with the personality that's already in place. If you do decide to get a puppy, get one no younger than 8-10 weeks. This is the beginning of the juvenile stage of development when they'll be fully weaned and ready to be separated from their mother.

One Pug or Two?

Pugs really enjoy the company of other dogs, and they love other Pugs especially. If you work during the day, two dogs can keep each other company, limiting problems with separation anxiety.

Two Pugs will take more work than one. You'll have to clean up twice as much shed hair, buy twice as much food, and expend twice the effort during housebreaking and training. This is the trade-off you'll have to consider, especially if you're buying puppies.

If you do get two dogs, a spayed female and neutered male are the best combination. It's ideal if you can get two puppies from the same litter. Watch them interact at the breeder and look for puppies that seem especially friendly with each other.

If you can't get Pugs from the same litter, you may want to consider staggering their homecomings. Get one puppy first and wait until he's completed basic obedience to get a second. You'll have to spend longer training, but it won't be as overwhelming as training two puppies at once.

The Right Pug for Your Family

Maybe the most important thing to figure out is what you're looking for from a companion. If you're not quite sure, spend some time thinking about it before choosing a breeder or shelter. Ask yourself questions like:

- **Do you have kids** (or plan to have kids within the Pug's lifetime)? Dogs with an even temperament tend to do best with infants and toddlers, especially.
- **Is your lifestyle more active or sedentary?** You should choose a Pug whose energy level matches yours.
- **Do you plan to show or breed your animal?** Your list of qualifications will be much more specific if this is the case.

While a puppy's personality isn't always set, you can tell a lot about how they'll develop by watching the parents. You should also tell the breeder what kind of temperament you're looking for. The breeder is more familiar with his or her Pugs than anyone else and will be able to steer you toward the right puppy.

CHAPTER 8

Preparing for Your Pug

B efore you rush out and buy your new Pug puppy, there are a few things you should do to prepare. You should get all the supplies you need before picking up your Pug puppy. That will keep you from having to rush out to the store when you'd rather be home helping your pup adjust.

There are a few things you'll want to do to your home, too, before there's a rambunctious Pug puppy running around. Proper preparation will assure that bringing your Pug home is exciting rather than stressful and will help you get your life together started on the best path.

The best dog harness for Pugs can be both stylish and comfortable.

Supplies

While a lot of the toys and treats you buy for your Pug are optional, there are some supplies that are definite necessities. At the very least, you'll need a kennel, a collar or harness, a leash, plus food and water dishes. You'll also want to pick up some nice toys for your energetic Pug puppy to play with. Let's go through each of these categories and talk about what's best for Pugs.

Pug kennels

Your Pug's kennel is a multi-purpose tool. It's a carrier for traveling and going to the vet, a safe space and refuge at home, and a nice place to nap. The right Pug kennel is also very helpful when you're housetraining.

The kennel should be just big enough for your Pug to stand up and turn around comfortably, but don't get one that's too big—you don't want him to go to the bathroom in the kennel and be able to move away from it. This might encourage future accidents.

Wire and plastic are the two main styles of crates. Wire crates are easier to fold up and store and give better ventilation. A plastic crate gives more security and is usually easier to carry.

Do you need a Pug dog bed?

Many people prefer to have their Pugs sleep in bed with them. In other cases, you can use your kennel as a safe, comfortable place for your Pug, in lieu of a dedicated bed. Pugs do like to be comfortable, however, so you may want to get a Pug bed for the room where he hangs out, or get a couple and put them in various rooms.

Collar vs. harness

A Pug harness is usually a better idea than a Pug collar. Collars put pressure on the neck, which can make breathing problems worse. The shape of a Pug's head also leads to the risk that they'll shrug a collar right off, especially when they're puppies.

The best harness for Pugs is one made for small dogs. Some harnesses, like the Pug Life all-in-one harness, are designed specifically for dogs with a broad chest. The best collars for Pugs are flat, buckle-style versions, about ¾" (2cm) wide and 12-16" (30-40cm) long. When you put it on, you should be able to slide two fingers comfortably under it—snug without being tight.

Don't forget to get an ID tag for your Pug dog harness or collar. You can have these personalized at most pet stores to include the pet's name, your name, and your phone number. This will make it much easier to find your Pug if he ever wanders off.

Along with your collar and harness, you'll need a Pug leash. Retractable and lockable leashes can be helpful in training your Pug. Pugs are known to be notorious pullers. The best harness for Pug puppy training still lets you guide your dog when you're walking.

Food and water dishes

A Pug's dishes should be durable and hard to move. Pugs tend to eat pretty aggressively and are likely to flip or push a flimsy bowl. The best shape is wide and low with a rounded bottom. Look for dishes with weighted or non-slip bases. You can also get bowls that go into a raised stand. These not only keep dishes well in place but are often more comfortable for a Pug to eat from, and can limit spilling.

Metals, like stainless steel, work well. They don't hold odors or bacteria and are easy to clean. They only disadvantage is they can't go in the microwave if you want to warm your Pug's food. Ceramic can be a good material since it's heavy, easy to clean, and microwave safe. Just be careful you don't break or chip it. Plastic bowls are inexpensive, but they are easier to damage and may trigger allergies in some Pugs.

What are good toys for Pugs?

Pug puppies are very energetic, so you'll want to have plenty of toys on-hand to entertain them. Pugs' favorite toys are fleece or plush stuffed animals. They're chewable and cuddly, satisfying both sides of the Pug's split personality. You'll want to get a lot of them—Pug puppies like to chew, and they'll go through soft toys faster than you might expect.

Classic squeak toys are often good toys for Pugs, too. They'll love to chase and chew them. Make sure to monitor the toy's condition, and dispose of it if the noisemaker in the middle is exposed. These can be choking hazards if the Pug manages to chew it loose.

Hard rubber chewing toys are some of the best toys for Pugs, especially as they enter adolescence. Chew toys made by Kong and similar companies can be filled with peanut butter or another tasty treat. These make an appealing alternative to shoes, furniture, and other options for the Pug's chew instinct. Generally, most Pugs will be more attracted to fuzzy toys than hard vinyl or rubber ones. Offer your puppy a variety of Pug chew toys and Pug dog plush toys, and see which ones they gravitate towards.

A plush or other stuffed animal makes a great toy for a Pug.

Puppy-proofing Basics

Puppies love to explore, and a Pug puppy can fit into surprisingly small spaces. Puppies also have a habit of exploring the world with their mouths, and this can be dangerous for them if you don't prepare properly.

Anything that's on the floor will be fair game for your Pug puppy. Thoroughly clean your home a few days before the puppy arrives. Run the vacuum, making sure to sweep under and behind all the furniture. If you have a habit of leaving clutter on the floor, you'll want to curtail that. Pug puppies can easily destroy shoes, books, or anything else left in their chewing area. At least until your Pug is trained, you'll want to keep a relatively clean house.

Once the floor is clear, turn your eyes a little higher. Anything within about 18" of the ground will catch your Pug's eye. Get down on the floor and look at things from the Pug's perspective. Move anything that could hurt the Pug if chewed and swallowed, like pens and pencils, or sewing materials. Don't forget to check under the beds and shift anything you don't want them getting into.

Some Pugs are smart enough; they learn to open low cabinet doors. You may want to consider getting small locks for the doors, especially cabinets where you keep food or cleaning supplies.

Power cords and cables can be especially dangerous for Pugs. Move them out of chewing range of your Pug if possible. You can also use PVC pipe to protect cords from your Pug's curious chewing.

Indoor and outdoor hazards

Many common house plants can be dangerous for your Pug. If you have any plants in your home, look them up on a poison control website to determine their toxicity. If they could be harmful, move them higher or dispose of them. Pugs are drawn to growing things and dirt in general. Any potted plant is likely to become the target of your Pug's curiosity. If you don't want it nibbled on or dug up, you should relocate it to a higher level.

If you have a garden, you should keep your Pug away from it. Just like house plants, many common garden plants can be toxic for dogs, including vegetable plants like tomato and flowers like daffodils and wisteria. Their digging can be destructive for the garden, as well, so it's often best to avoid the situation.

Other things in your home that could be dangerous to Pugs include:

- **Pools and hot tubs.** Supervise your Pug any time he's around an open pool or hot tub to make sure he doesn't fall in. It's also good to cover them when they're not in use If there are natural ponds in your yard, a fence can prevent accidents.

- **Garages.** There are a lot of hazards in most garages, ranging from tools and small hardware to automotive chemicals. Leaked oil or transmission fluid can make your Pug sick if he licks them, and less than a tablespoon of antifreeze can kill a Pug if ingested. If you plan to use your garage as a space for your Pug, clean it thoroughly first to make sure it's safe.

- **Medications.** Even a small amount of human medication can be very bad for dogs. This includes over the counter products like pain relievers and cold medicine. Make sure there are no loose pills lying around and keep bottles of medication out of your Pug's reach.
- **Cleaning products.** Chemicals like bleach are harmful if ingested. Don't leave used sponges and rags lying around, either, where your Pug might chew on them.
- **Trash cans.** Discarded food can be very appealing to a Pug, but there's a lot of stuff in the trash they shouldn't have. Make sure all trash cans, even those in bathrooms and laundry rooms, are covered securely.

Establishing a Schedule

Dogs thrive on routine, and it's especially important for a potentially stubborn breed like the Pug. You can get a head start on your Pug's routine before he even comes home. Decide as a family who will be responsible for which aspects of the Pug's care. If there are multiple people who will be feeding him, you may want to get a calendar to track his daily meals—Pugs are great at conning their way into extra meals.

If you're buying the Pug as a pet for kids, make sure there's a system in place to hold them accountable. Your Pug's health is more important than teaching your child a lesson about responsibility. If his care is being neglected, it's your job to step in and correct it.

Registering Your Pug

Even if you don't plan to show your animal, there are advantages to registering him with a local breed club. This will be an additional resource you can draw on if your Pug is lost. You won't be able to officially register your Pug until you bring him home, but you can reach out to local breed clubs and get all the forms and paperwork together in advance.

You should also think about whether you want to have your dog microchipped or tattooed. A microchip is inserted under the skin and will help return a lost Pug to you if he ends up with a vet or shelter. Tattooing is similar, but puts a visible identification number permanently on your dog, usually on the inner thigh. This has the advantage of being readable by those without a reader. Whichever way you go, you'll want to do it early, so it's a good thing to think about before you bring your Pug home.

CHAPTER 9

Bringing Your Pug Home

Introducing your Pug puppy to his new home is exciting—but it can also be stressful and intimidating, especially if this is your first puppy. Preparing in advance using the steps in the last chapter is one way to keep the day stress-free for both you and your Pug. Even so, it's likely to be a frenetic day.

Plan carefully when you'll be bringing your Pug puppy home. If possible, do it when you have a couple days home from work or school. This will let you supervise the puppy and will speed your bonding. Pugs love to be around people, so it will help your puppy adjust to having you home, too.

Expect your curious Pug puppy to explore everything when you bring him home.

Pick up your Pug when the house is calm. Holidays aren't a great time to introduce a new animal to the house. If it's already hectic with people coming and going, there will be less time and energy to devote to your Pug. You want the environment to be calm, letting your Pug meet his new family before you open him up to new experiences. If you want to give a Pug as a birthday or Christmas present, consider gifting a symbolic item, like a toy or a collar, then going together to pick up the Pug after things have calmed down.

Picking Up Your Pug Puppy

The breeder will have a few things for you when you pick up your Pug. Along with the dog's paperwork and pedigree, they'll usually send you home with a small portion of their current puppy food. Make sure to ask the breeder any last questions you have about the puppy's eating habits, training, and care. It's also helpful to get something that has the scent of the mom on it, like a cloth or a toy. Putting this in the Pug puppy's kennel for the ride can make it less stressful.

Bring your Pug kennel with you when you go to the breeder. Line the kennel with a soft blanket or towel and put a plush toy inside for the Pug to snuggle with on the ride home. Put the Pug in the kennel before you leave the breeder, and leave him in it until you've gotten home. Nerves can make your Pug sick or may make him pee. He might also be excitable and hard to hold on to. It's much safer for him to ride in his crate in the back seat. If you're worried he'll be lonely, have someone sit on the seat beside the crate, and talk softly to the Pug through the carrier.

Once you're home, grab your Pug's collar and leash, and take him to his pee spot before going inside. Puppies go to the bathroom a lot, so he'll almost certainly have to go. Let the Pug sniff around, but don't go for a long walk, yet—just enough time for him to relieve himself. Praise him a lot when he goes to start building a positive association with peeing outside.

The First Day

You'll probably find it easiest to isolate the Pug puppy in a single room or another isolated area the first day. This makes the new space less overwhelming for the Pug, who will be adjusting to a whole new host of sounds and smells. It also makes it easier to isolate the Pug from other animals, small kids, or potential hazards.

Your Pug's training and socialization starts on the day you bring him home. The earlier you establish the house rules and set yourself up as the alpha, the easier it will be to train and housebreak your Pug. Continue to give him lots of praise when he goes out to the bathroom. Do the same to encourage other positive behaviors, and use distraction rather than correction to deal with chewing or barking.

There will need to be a few more bathroom trips throughout the first day. Puppies usually have to go out after meals, after naps, and before bedtime, but it's not always predictable. Take him out every couple of hours, even if he doesn't seem antsy. If you see the puppy start to go, get him outside if you can. Otherwise, calmly clean up the accident and try to catch him quicker next time.

Even if you plan to have the Pug sleep in your bed, you should have him sleep in his kennel until he's housebroken. You can move the kennel into your room overnight—he'll likely be reassured by your smell. Don't let him out of his kennel if he cries. You don't want to teach him that whining is productive. Comfort him from outside the kennel, instead.

Pugs are a very adaptable breed. It usually only takes them a couple days to make your home their own. Spend most of the time, your first couple days, playing—this will help you bond, and the attention will keep him from missing his littermates. If he's shy at first, don't force him to interact. Sit calmly in his space and let the Pug decide when he wants to come to you. Puppies take a lot of naps, too. If you notice him getting tired, encourage him to go to his kennel, and make sure everyone in the house gives him some time to sleep.

Your Pug's First Vet Visit

You'll want to take your new Pug puppy to the vet within the first couple weeks of bringing him home. The vet can answer any lingering questions you have and make sure your care and feeding are on the right track. They'll also consult with you about any future vaccinations or pest treatments that are needed.

The first vet visit will set the tone for the future. Pugs learn quickly, and you don't want them to learn that "vet" is a bad word. Make the first visit an exam only, with no shots or immunizations. Give your Pug a lot of praise, and bring his favorite toys and treats. Keep your Pug in his kennel in the waiting room. You can bring him in on his leash in the future, but until he's socialized and vaccinated, it's best to avoid interactions with other animals.

Socializing Pug Puppies

Pugs are naturally friendly, so socializing them is normally a breeze. Like many things, it starts the first day your Pug comes home. Encourage him to explore new things. Once he's settled in, you can have friends come by to visit the puppy, introducing him to a variety of people and smells. When you go out on walks, encourage people to play with and pet him so he gets used to strangers.

Socializing is also about introducing your Pug to his world, and this means new environments as well as new people. Make sure he walks on a variety of surfaces, including grates, gravel, sand, and other potentially tricky terrains. The more new experiences your Pug has when he's young, the better-adjusted he'll be as an adult.

Introducing Pugs to other animals

If there are other animals living in your home, it's a judgment call when to introduce them to the new Pug. Some Pugs will be ready after two days; some may need a couple of weeks. Even though they've been isolated, your other animals' smells are still all over your house (and you). This familiarity usually makes these introductions easier. The exception to this is if you have outdoor cats. Wait to make those introductions until the Pug is fully-vaccinated, as you would with any animal that lives outside the home.

When it comes to introducing your Pug to outside animals, it's best to start with other dogs, ideally other small dogs. Have a play session with your Pug first, so he's less energetic. Make the introduction on neutral territory, so neither animal feels dominant. Don't force the dogs to interact, and keep them both on a leash at first. If either dog seems overly frightened or aggressive, separate them and give it a rest.

When introducing a Pug to a cat, keep the Pug contained and let the cat roam at will. You may want to keep your Pug in his kennel at first and let the cat sniff and explore around the kennel before opening the door. For friendlier cats, putting the Pug on the leash should be enough.

Once your puppy has met a few dogs, the dog park is a great place to expand his experiences. Bring plenty of water, and pay attention to the weather—limit sessions to the morning and evening in the summer, and look for a dog park with plenty of shade. Always keep a close watch on your Pug when he's playing with other dogs, and keep him on a leash until he's fully trained, even in an enclosed park.

Fear reactions

Minor fear reactions are normal for any puppy—everything in the world is new, after all. You don't want your Pug to get in the habit of being fearful, though. A fearful puppy can become a territorial or excitable adult.

The key is to not reward a fear reaction. If your Pug puppy starts to bark at the blender or the vacuum cleaner, calmly tell the dog that it's okay and encourage him to explore it further. Don't immediately begin to comfort him—this reinforces the fear reaction. Save your affection for after he's investigated the offending object, so he associates praise with overcoming fear.

Overcoming fear reactions is especially important for Pugs that live in the city. You don't want him to bolt every time he hears a car horn or a loud truck. Start introducing your Pug to city noises early. You can take him for walks in his kennel until he's old enough to be trusted on a leash. The sooner he gets used to crowds and traffic, the safer he'll be on his walks.

Socializing Adult Pugs

Socializing a new adult Pug is often easier than socializing a puppy. The problem with adult dogs is that you don't know what experiences they've had. An adult Pug who's never met a cat may be more resistant to it than a puppy, so you need to be careful with your introductions.

You can gauge your new Pug's level of familiarity with other dogs by taking him on a trip to the dog park. See how he reacts to different breeds and sizes of dogs. If he seems mostly outgoing and friendly, he's probably been well-socialized. On the other hand, if your Pug seems afraid, aggressive, or shy, you may need to take a step back and make a one-on-one introduction. Let your Pug dictate his engagement with other animals until you're sure what he's comfortable with.

CHAPTER 10

The Best Pug Dog Diet

G oing to the pet store for dog food can be pretty overwhelming. There are so many different varieties, brands, and recipes—and a lot of them claim to be the best for your animal. But which is the best food for Pugs— and is the best Pug puppy diet the same thing you'll feed adults?

You can't always count on your puppy to know the best dog food for Pugs.

While there is no one diet that will be best for every puppy, we've got some tips on finding the best diet for Pugs at every stage of their life. We'll also go through all the different kinds of food that you can buy, as well as the pros and cons of each. Consider it your map to navigating the pet store's shelves.

What is the Best Pug Dog Food?

As a rule, Pugs aren't picky eaters. To a Pug, "favorite food" usually means whatever is in front of them. This makes your job as an owner easier. You can focus on making your Pug's diet healthy, and in most cases, your little guy will gobble it up happily.

Many commercial dog foods can make an ideal Pug dog diet, but there are also some you should avoid. Always read the label on any Pug dog food. Look for a food that has animal protein as the first two to three ingredients. This can be poultry, beef, pork, fish, or even exotic meats, like venison or buffalo—the exact animal doesn't matter as much as the protein and other nutrients. As far as brands, there are many brands that could contend for the title best dog food for Pugs.

While the naming of Pug food can be hard to decipher, it is tightly regulated in the USA. If a dog food is labeled with just a meat name, at least 95% of the food must be that meat. The same goes for multi-protein foods; if it says "beef and chicken," it has to be a total of 95% beef and chicken, with the beef making up a higher portion. If there is another word added to the food's name (e.g., dinner, platter, entrée, nuggets, etc.), the food only has to contain 25% of the named protein.

Pugs do need carbohydrates, as well as fats and proteins. Some grain in your dog's food is actually good for them. The key is to find the right balance. The form the food takes doesn't matter as long as it's nutritious. Let's look at the most popular varieties.

Dry food

Dry dog foods are the most economical and convenient option. Quality dry food can be an ideal Pug diet. It has a relatively long shelf life, so you can buy it in bulk. For a Pug, you want to choose the smallest kibble size available.

The main disadvantage of dry dog food is that it's not as tasty for the animal, although this isn't usually a concern for Pugs. Nutritionally, it has a good balance of fat and protein but may contain too many carbohydrates. The specific carbohydrates used may aggravate some Pug allergies, which are most likely to be caused by things like wheat and corn.

Canned food

Canned food is a bit more expensive than dry food. It also has a higher water content, which means it's not as nutritionally dense as dry food. While it has a long shelf life when unopened, it will spoil within a few days once you crack the can.

Nutritionally, it often has a higher fat content, which may be bad for a Pug that's prone to weight problems. Canned food can be the best dog food for senior Pugs since it's easier to eat and digest. Steer clear of canned foods that contain a lot of sugar. These are more like junk food and best reserved for treats.

Frozen food

Frozen foods are the most natural commercial pet food option. They use fresh ingredients, and since they're kept cold, they don't require preservatives. Because they're targeted at serious dog owners, the nutritional balance is usually spot on. The disadvantage here is price and convenience. It's the most expensive commercial Pug diet. It might also be tricky to find, especially in rural areas.

Homemade Foods

The idea of making your Pug's food might be appealing, but it's a bit more complicated than you might imagine. You don't just want to feed your Pug the same things you eat, for one. Human food often has spices and flavorings that aren't good for dogs, and a Pug's nutritional needs are different from a human diet. If you're preparing a homemade diet, you'll want to make something specifically for the Pug.

A homemade diet takes more effort than any other option. You'll want to work with your vet to achieve the right balance of protein, vegetables, and grains, or other carbohydrates. For most Pug owners, a homemade diet is more trouble than it's worth, though it is the best healthy food for pugs with dietary allergies.

Pug Raw Diet

The extreme form of the homemade diet is the Pug raw diet. Many dog owners assume a raw diet is healthier since it's what the animal would eat in the wild, but there is no scientific evidence that it's better than any high-quality dog food.

Be cautious with what meat you use if you choose to use a raw diet for your Pug. Don't assume the meat in the grocery store is safe. Things like ground beef and chicken breasts are intended to be cooked and may contain harmful bacteria. Look for tartare-grade beef, sushi-grade fish—high-quality meats intended to be eaten raw.

What is the Best Pug Puppy Diet?

When you first bring your puppy home, you should feed them the same thing they ate at the breeder. This is likely to be a good Pug puppy food, first of all. The consistency also helps the puppy adjust to their new home. Many breeders will give you a bag of food, or have food for sale on-site. If not, they'll at least be able to tell you what it is so you can buy your own.

Keep your puppy on this original food for about two weeks. If you decide to change to a different Pug puppy dog food at this point, do it gradually. Mix the new food in with the old for 1-2 weeks, gradually shifting the balance to be more new and less old.

The best food for your Pug puppy is one labeled for growth or a puppy-specific formula of food for small dogs. Pug puppies often switch to an adult food earlier than other breeds and may be ready for adult food as early as 10-12 weeks. Check with your vet to see what they recommend for your pug.

Best Dog Food for Overweight Pugs

Obesity is a serious concern for Pugs. If you notice your Pug is getting a bit chubby, it's often better to change your type of food rather than reducing the amount. The best dog food for overweight Pugs is one that's low in fat. Avoid canned and semi-moist foods, sticking to low-calorie dry foods, or raw and homemade diets based on lean animal proteins, like fish.

Healthy Snacks for a Pug

When it comes to treats, you want to look for things that are low in calories and high in flavor. Fruits and vegetables often make great healthy snacks for Pugs since they're high in fiber and nutritionally dense. If you'd rather buy commercial treats, stick to ones made for small dogs, and follow the same rules as with Pug food: make sure animal protein is the main ingredient, and avoid anything with lots of sugar or artificial flavorings.

Limit treats to 5-10% of your Pug's daily diet. About 1-2 tablespoons per day is good for an adult Pug. It's often better to give many small treats throughout the day. Your Pug will be excited to receive a treat, no matter how big it is.

What Shouldn't You Feed Your Pug?

Most pugs really love to eat, so you can't always trust them to make the best choices for themselves. There are some foods that are a bad idea for Pugs (or dogs in general). These include:

- **Chocolate.** The sugar and fat content of chocolate makes it suspect, but they're not even the main concern. Cacao contains a chemical called theobromine that is toxic to dogs. The darker the chocolate, the more it contains. Even a small amount can be dangerous to a Pug.

- **Onions and garlic.** These pervasive vegetables are healthy for humans but have chemicals that can destroy a dog's red blood cells, leading to anemia and other health problems.

- **Grapes or raisins.** Not all dogs have a problem with raisins and grapes, but for some, they can cause kidney failure. It's best to avoid them entirely. If your Pug accidentally eats a raisin, monitor him carefully, and take him to the vet if he starts to throw up or have diarrhea.

- **Alcohol, caffeine, and tobacco.** You should never give any intoxicant to your dog. Beer and caffeinated soda are especially bad because they contain sugars and carbonation, in addition to harmful chemicals.

- **Green tomatoes and raw potatoes.** While the ripe, cooked versions of these foods are fine, both raw potatoes and green tomatoes contain potentially toxic chemicals.

- **Avocados.** Avocados naturally contain persin, which is a toxin that prevents fungus from attacking the plant and is contained in the leaves, pits, and fruit. This can also be toxic to dogs, however, sometimes even leading to death.

CHAPTER 11

Raising Your Pug: From Puppy to Adult

Compared to other breeds, there isn't as much of a difference between a Pug puppy and a full-grown Pug. While they do calm as they age, like most dogs, Pugs maintain a puppy-like playfulness and curiosity well into adulthood—one of the reasons they're so popular.

There is also a lot of individual variation in the temperament of different Pugs as they age. You'll want to carefully observe your puppy's behavior. Combined with what you observed from the parents at the breeder, this will be your best indication of what to expect from your adult Pug.

Generally speaking, though, most Pugs will calm a bit as they age. Once they reach the 2-year mark, their energy level will diminish somewhat, and you'll notice your Pug is more content to sit with you on the couch. This is also the point you can expect to leave your Pug at home alone unsupervised, although some will adapt to this much earlier. Even so, expect your Pug to be constantly exploring. Many Pugs will love their chew toys as much in adulthood as they did when they were puppies.

*The right Pug toy is key in keeping your puppy entertained—
and is beloved by many Pug adults, too.*

Pug Life Stages

Unless you're raising a newborn Pug puppy, you'll likely miss the
first few stages of its life, which are very quick and happen before
the puppy is weaned from its mother. By 8-10 weeks old, a Pug
puppy is independent enough to eat and go to the bathroom on
his own and can be separated safely from his litter.

This stage of puppyhood lasts a bit longer—up to when the Pug
is 6 months of age. Your Pug is growing very quickly during this
time, so he'll need a lot of food. He'll also have a very erratic
energy level, going between hyper and bouncy and passed out on
the floor in no time flat. Providing a good balance of exercise and
sleep is especially important during these early months to make
sure your Pug puppy is developing properly. Avoid making the

Pug jump or take long walks, so you don't damage his developing skeletal system.

From around 6 to 18 months, your Pug will be in its adolescent stage. This is when you'll see the majority of problem behaviors. The puppy will be very likely to chew on things and may be more destructive than he was as a puppy now that he feels more confident exploring his environment. You should also expect him to have periodic accidents in the house, even if he's mostly housebroken.

By the 18 month mark, your Pug will be basically full-grown, and you can treat him as an adult in regard to care and feeding. By this point, they'll usually chew and bark less, although these can be life-long behaviors. Some Pugs do take as long as 2 years to mellow into their adult temperament, especially if they were particularly energetic puppies.

Adult and Puppy Pug Feeding

Pugs aren't especially good at regulating their own food intake. Most of them love food—as much of it as they can eat. As the owner, it's up to you to regulate your Pug's portions, so he doesn't become overweight. Obesity is especially bad for puppies, impeding the development of their bones and muscles, so you'll want to monitor how much your Pug puppy is eating carefully as he grows.

The amount of food your Pug needs every day will gradually increase until he reaches about 18 months old, and then will drop once he's reached his adult size. Every Pug is different, so make sure you're monitoring his weight and adjusting his food intake accordingly. As a general guideline, you can use the Pug feeding chart below:

Age	Amount	Times/Day
2-3 months	¼-½ cup	4
3-6 months	1/3- ½ cup	3
6-18 months	½-¾ cup	2
Adult	½ cup	2

Bathroom Routine: Puppies vs. Adults

When you first bring your Pug puppy home, he'll need to go out a lot—every two hours, at least. You'll take them out as soon as they wake up in the morning, after every meal and nap, and before they go into the kennel at night. As your Pug ages, however, he'll be able to hold his bladder for longer, and the time between walks can increase.

A good rule of thumb is that the frequency of your Pug puppy's bathroom trips is equal to their age in months. A 3-month-old puppy should be taken out every three hours, a 6-month-old puppy, every 6 hours, and so on. By adulthood, you can take your Pug out in the morning, before bed, and after each meal.

Exercise

For most Pugs, a bit of light exercise every day is the healthiest option. Pugs aren't particularly athletic breeds, so they don't need strenuous exercise—in other words, don't expect them to gallop after a thrown stick. In fact, seeing a Pug running is pretty rare. Most Pugs aren't big fans of fetch and chase games, though there are some who will gladly take off after a squirrel or cat when spotted.

Finding a good Pug puppy harness is important when you're taking a young Pug for a walk. Even in fenced areas, like dog parks, you don't want to let your Pug get off-leash exercise until he's trained.

If pressed, the sturdy Pug can walk up to 5 miles once it's an adult. You shouldn't push him to do this too often, though. Pay attention to the weather when you take your Pug for walks, too. Pugs are very sensitive to heat and will get tired more easily in warm weather. Indoor play is a fine substitute for walks when it comes to getting exercise, especially on days the weather outside isn't cooperating.

Regular walks are an important part of a Pug's routine at any stage in his life.

Overcoming Separation Anxiety

As we mentioned before, some Pugs cope well with being left alone, even as puppies. Others will bond very closely with their people, however, and can get lonely if left to their own devices.

If your Pug whines, barks, or becomes destructive when you leave him alone, there are a few things you can do to help relieve his separation anxiety. First, remember that dogs, in general, are very sensitive to human emotions. It's possible you're nervous about leaving your Pug alone, and he's picking up on those vibes. Make your departure less of an event. Give your Pug a little less attention before you leave, and gather your things up calmly. Do the same when you return: greet your Pug calmly rather than making a big fuss over him, and wait until you've been at home for a little while to feed him or have playtime.

Some Pug owners find it helpful to establish a signal that they're about to leave. This lets the Pug know he's about to be left alone and can reduce his anxiety. This can be as simple as picking up and shaking your keys—just as long as it's something you do every time you leave, and only when you leave.

Finally, get your Pug used to being left alone gradually. Start by stepping out for a few minutes at a time. Do this a few times throughout the day, so that your Pug can see you always come back when you leave. Once he is able to calmly handle your absence for short periods, extend the amount of time that you leave.

A companion can also help to ease your Pug's loneliness. If you're out of the house for long periods, consider a second dog or another animal, like a cat or rabbit, that the Pug can interact with when you're not home.

Pug Travel Tips

A Pug's small size makes them an easier travel companion than bigger breeds—and they're generally much more laid-back during travel than most small breeds. Most Pugs enjoy rides in the car. Make sure you keep your Pug in his kennel in the backseat until he's fully-trained—a rambunctious Pug can be a big distraction for a driver.

Some Pugs do get motion sickness. Signs of this include whining, drooling, yawning, and vomiting during car rides. Rolling the window down can help, but never let your Pug stick his head out of the window, which can be dangerous. If this motion sickness doesn't go away with time, you can get medication from your vet to ease his symptoms when you need to take him on a trip.

If you'll be taking your Pug on a lot of car rides and don't want to keep him in his kennel every time, it's advised to get a puppy seat belt. These products are relatively inexpensive and offer extra protection for your Pug in case of an accident. Also, make sure your Pug is always on his leash on his way to and from the car, even if you're just loading him up in your home driveway. Pugs can be surprisingly swift when they want to be, and a moment of distraction can be all it takes to lose sight of him.

For air travel, you'll want to get a Fiberglas or plastic kennel that's approved by airlines. You can find these clearly-labeled in any pet store. Most Pugs are small enough to fit easily in kennels that go under the seat in front of you, so you can normally keep them in the cabin with you rather than loading them below with the larger animals.

CHAPTER 12

Pug Training

The training you give your Pug puppy goes beyond being able to show off tricks for friends. Proper training is an important part of any happy long-term pet/owner relationship—and it starts from the first time you bring your Pug home.

Training your Pug is usually an easy process. If given the proper motivation (usually food), a Pug puppy will learn commands faster than many breeds, thanks to their combination of intelligence and desire to please their humans. Pugs do have a stubborn streak too, though, so training a Pug puppy can have its challenges.

Training your Pug can be fun for both of you.

This chapter will get you started on your Pug training. It covers the bare minimum you'll need for a family pet, from house training a Pug puppy to training a Pug to sit and stay. Once your Pug has mastered everything in this Pug book about training, you can decide if you want to take things to the next level.

Are Pugs Easy to Train?

Normally, yes. This is true the entire way from the basics up through advanced competitive routines. The key is to know how to interact with a Pug. The more you try to force a Pug to obey, the more obstinate it's likely to become. Positive reinforcement works exceptionally well, especially if you're using food as a motivation.

You can get lots of Pug puppy training tips from breeders, but ultimately it comes down to repetition. With enough practice over enough time, your Pug can master a surprising range of skills.

Pug Puppy Crate Training

Crate training a Pug is the best starting point for future endeavors. It's you and your Pug's first exercise in using positive reinforcement to encourage good behavior. Crate training also lays the groundwork for future training by establishing you as the alpha of your Pug's pack.

Start your Pug puppy crate training by making the kennel a place your dog wants to be. You can sprinkle treats in it the first few days. After that, make it appealing by keeping it warm and comfortable, or by providing your Pug's favorite toys. Praise your Pug any time he goes into the kennel of his own accord, especially during his first few days home.

A crate can be a good time-out spot for a rambunctious Pug, but you shouldn't use it as a punishment tool. Never scold your Pug while you're putting him in the crate. You'll only build negative associations with the crate itself, not with the behavior that prompted it.

Pug Potty Training

Shortly after crate training comes Pug potty training. House training a Pug is a bit more difficult than you'd expect, given their reputation as quick learners. It mostly comes from the Pug's independence—they're not a breed that wants to be told when and where to do their business.

Your best tools for housebreaking a Pug are a crate and a consistent routine. Ideally, someone should be at home and able to take the Pug puppy out for walks every two to three hours during the housebreaking process. The more consistently the Pug does his business outside, the quicker he'll understand he shouldn't go in the house.

If you can't be home during the day, expect the housebreaking process to be a bit slower. Don't simply keep your Pug locked up in his crate all day. The best option is to close off a space with a fence or indoor playpen. Line the floor with pee pads or newspaper, and provide your Pug with his food and water dish. It's ideal if you can position this area near to the door where you'll take the Pug out, firmly establishing this area as the place to go when he has to pee.

Consistency is important when housebreaking a Pug. Take him to the same place to pee every time he goes out, and do it around the same time of day. This will help his internal clock to get on track with yours. Feeding your Pug at the same time every day will help, too—your Pug will naturally have to go to the bathroom about 15-20 minutes after eating.

Give your Pug lots of praise when he goes to the bathroom outside. If you come home to an accident, don't scold your Pug. This won't help your Pug house training efforts; by the time you see the accident, the Pug has already forgotten about it, and won't know what he's being scolded for. Simply clean up the mess with a deodorizing spray. You can buy urine-specific cleaners at the pet store, though carpet cleaning sprays work well, too.

You can start housebreaking a Pug in earnest once they're around 6 months old. This is the point at which they can fully hold their bladders. In some cases, Pugs can take 6 months to a year to master house training, and some are never fully housebroken reliably, even Pugs that are adept at learning other commands.

Some Pugs do take well to litter box training, which can be an attractive prospect for those who live in colder climates. If you want to experiment with this, you should wait until the Pug is an adult and fully-housebroken. Trying to housebreak and litterbox-train a Pug at the same time sends mixed signals and makes it less likely your dog will learn either. Litterbox training can be a viable alternative if you have a Pug who refuses to be housebroken, as well.

Leash Training

Pugs are both curious and strong-willed. This makes them bad leash walkers unless they get the right training. Just like with housebreaking, there are no Pug training secrets. You just have to consistently reinforce the right way until your Pug decides to go along with it.

If your Pug tends to tug on his leash every time you walk him, you may want to use a collar rather than a harness for the training. This makes it easier to control where your dog is walking in relation to you. You can switch back to a harness if you'd like once he's mastered the command.

Start leash training from your first walk with your Pug. Whenever he pulls, rushes ahead, or tries to chase something, tug gently on the leash and tell the Pug to "heel" or "walk pretty," whichever term you prefer. When he complies, give him a lot of praise, and occasionally a treat reward. Over time, the desire for rewards will override his natural instinct to run off and explore.

Even an energetic Pug can learn to walk calmly with time.

Basic commands

There are three basic commands every dog should know: sit, stay, and down. Before we get into the nitty-gritty of each skill, let's go through some basic Pug training tips.

The most important thing is to keep the training sessions fun for your dog. Do your Pug dog training when both of you are in a good mood. With puppies, it's often a good idea to have some playtime or a walk first to get rid of some energy and help your Pug to focus.

Your training sessions should be short and uninterrupted. Keep them to around 5-10 minutes at a time for puppies. Turn off the TV and remove any Pug distractions, like toys, food, or other animals.

Everyone who's going to be giving the Pug commands regularly should be part of the training process. For young kids, Pug training is a chance to learn the right way to handle the puppy, so you should involve them even if you're doing most of the actual training.

Pay attention to the tone of voice you use when you're training, too. Use a higher-pitched, happy voice for praise, and a firm, low voice when you're giving commands. This will help your Pug puppy pick up on what you're teaching.

The type of reward you use can make a difference, too. Most Pugs will be eager to perform for a tasty treat. Foods that smell good will be best since they'll be more enticing to your dog. If your Pug isn't responding to your Pug training efforts, try switching to a different reward until you find one he loves. If a reward used to work, but now your Pug is breaking commands or not responding, try going back a few steps in the training. He may just be a bit overwhelmed.

Finally, make sure that every session ends on a high note. If you're working on something that your Pug hasn't gotten down yet, go back to an earlier skill he knows and end with that. You always want training sessions to end in praise and treats, so your puppy looks forward to training time.

Training a Pug to sit

Sitting is a natural movement for a dog, and that makes this command fairly easy to teach. Hold a treat in one hand with your Pug in front of you. Raise your hand up slowly. Following the treat will automatically make the Pug sit. When his butt hits the ground, say "Good sit!" and give the treat and lots of praise. Once your Pug has done this a few times consistently, use just the voice command without the hand motion. Eventually, you can intersperse food rewards with praise rewards, working toward praise rewards only as the skill is mastered.

Stay and down

Once your Pug has mastered sit, he's ready for "stay" and "down." These commands are a bit harder because they work against a Pug's natural instincts. For stay, start by having your Pug sit, then put your palm up, and in your command voice, say, "Stay." Back up a few inches and wait a few seconds. If he's still sitting, say "Good stay!" and give him a treat. If he moves before you give the command, put him back, and start over. Gradually lengthen the distance between you, and the amount of time before you give the praise.

Once stay is mastered, you can work on down. This is the most difficult of the basic commands because it's putting your Pug in a submissive posture—something the Alpha-minded Pug tends to avoid. Start from sitting, then put a treat in front of your Pug's nose and lower it between his legs and forward. Say "Good down!" once he's laying down, and give treats and praise. Like with sit, you can lose the hand motion after he starts to get it and switch to praise-only rewards after a few successes.

Correcting Unwanted Behaviors

Most Pugs don't develop serious behavioral issues, or what you might think of as problem behavior. The best way to deal with unwanted behaviors is to prevent them by enforcing the rules consistently from the beginning.

One helpful command most Pug owners will want to teach their dogs is "Off." Pugs love people and are known to jump up and demand attention from strangers as well as friends. Since Pugs are small, most people don't mind them jumping up as much as bigger breeds—and that can make it even harder to train, since most people will pet and praise a Pug who jumps up on them, inadvertently rewarding the bad behavior.

Once your Pug knows "Sit," you may be able to distract him from jumping with this command. Many Pugs need a designated command, however. If the Pug jumps up, say "Off" and move his front paws to the floor. Once all four paws are on the floor, say "Good off!" and give a treat or praise reward. The goal is for the Pug to associate "Off" with having all four paws down. Once the command is mastered, it can also be used to steer the Pug away from furniture you don't want him sitting on.

Biting and chewing

Chewing on things is natural for a puppy. Pug puppy biting is more about exploring the world than causing harm, but you still need him to know it's not an okay thing to do. If your puppy nips you during play, pull your hand away and say "Ouch" in the command voice.

With chewing, it's more about teaching the Pug what's okay to chew on and what's not. The first step is to provide plenty of good chew toys. If you notice your Pug chewing on something he shouldn't, give a firm "No" command. Once his attention has been diverted from the object, find an approved chewing toy and offer it, then praise the Pug when he begins to chew. This will help him understand the difference between good chewing and bad chewing.

Limiting barking

Pugs aren't known to bark just for the sake of it. If your Pug is barking, there's a reason. Finding the source and distracting him from it is the best way to stop it. Don't yell at your Pug if he's barking. To the dog, this sounds like you're joining in, and he may even bark more. Instead, calmly acknowledge your Pug, then after a couple barks say "Enough" or "Quiet." When he stops barking, say "Good quiet," and give praise. Teaching the "Quiet" command can help you limit the barking.

Preventing begging

Un-training begging is very difficult. Your best bet is to not let the habit develop in the first place. This starts by never giving your puppy food from your plate. If he's received scraps of your meals or what you're cooking, of course, your Pug will come around looking for more. You may find it helpful to schedule your Pug's dinner and yours at the same time. This way, you're all eating together. If you do give your Pug human food, act like it's a treat. Give it to your Pug outside of human mealtimes, and have him perform a command before receiving it.

Puppy Kindergarten

If you're having difficulty training your Pug—or just want the guidance of an expert—you may want to consider training classes. They'll teach all the basics, including how to walk well on a leash. As an added bonus, your puppy will be able to socialize with other dogs during the training sessions.

Most puppy training classes have age restrictions on both the upper and lower end. You'll also need to show your puppy is fully vaccinated before he'll be allowed to participate. If you're interested, check with your local pet stores and breed clubs to find out when the next ones are taking place.

CHAPTER 13

Pug Health

While most Pugs are healthy and hearty, like all purebreds they have some genetic diseases that you'll want to be aware of. Making sure you have a healthy Pug means keeping an eye out for trouble signs and knowing when it's time for a trip to the vet.

In terms of non-hereditary health concerns, the most significant one for the Pug is obesity. An overweight Pug can have serious heart, joint, and breathing problems, especially as it ages. Along with this, you'll want to prevent the ailments common to all dogs, like parasites and illnesses. Preventative treatment goes a long way toward avoiding problems and giving your Pug as many healthy years as possible.

The right vet is an important piece of your Pug's overall health.

Finding a Vet

Your vet is your first line of defense against health problems, so you want to make sure you find the right one. The best way to find a good Pug vet is to ask the experts: Pug breeders and other Pug owners. Since it's such a common breed, you shouldn't have difficulty finding a vet in your area who's familiar with Pugs.

How often should you visit?

Initially, your vet will tell you when to bring your puppy in. You'll see the vet a lot more in your Pug's first year of life than in most of the years after. How often (and how much you'll pay) depends on whether you need to spay or neuter your Pug, and how far along they are with vaccinations.

Once he's an adult, you should take your Pug to the vet once a year for a check-up. This is also when he'll get any necessary boosters or vaccinations. After the age of 7, you may want to raise this to twice a year, so that you can catch any age-related issues before they become serious.

Signs of a problem

We've talked about scheduled vet visits—but what about the unexpected ones? Paying close attention to your Pug's behavior and physical condition is the best way to know when a vet visit is needed. Your weekly grooming sessions are a great time to check your Pug's eyes, ears, and teeth. Monitor how much he's eating, too, and take note of any sudden changes.

Common signs of health problems in Pugs include:

- Loss of appetite
- Sudden weight loss or weight gain
- Excessive urination, or a sudden break in house training
- Difficulty urinating or reduced frequency of urination
- Diarrhea or loose stools
- Vomiting
- Thick discharge from eyes or eyes
- Swollen or red eyes or ears
- Bad odor in breath or from ears
- Temperature over 103°F (40C)
- Frequent scratching or biting
- Dull or patchy coat

- Flaky or red patches on the skin
- Wheezing or labored breathing
- Limping, stiff movements or difficulty walking

These symptoms, alone or in combination, can point to a variety of ailments or injuries. Don't turn to the Internet and try to self-diagnose your animal. Contact your vet and find out what you can do to fix the problem. Keep the number for your vet, as well as the contact for poison control, in the same place you keep other emergency numbers.

Vaccinations

The modern vaccination suggestion for puppies is usually a three-shot sequence. Called the DAPP vaccine, it protects against the four most common canine viruses: distemper, adenovirus, parvovirus, and parainfluenza. The first shot is normally given by the breeder, at around 6-8 weeks old. The next should occur 3-4 weeks later, with the final shot 3-4 weeks after the second.

In most countries, you will also need to get your Pug a rabies shot. The notable exception is the United Kingdom, where rabies is not a significant concern. UK Pug owners will only need to get their dog a rabies shot for international travel. The rabies vaccine is typically given at around 16 weeks and is often administered alongside the last shot of the DAPP vaccine. In areas where rabies is common, you may be recommended to administer a rabies booster every three years.

There are other vaccines that you may want to consider, depending on where you live and your Pug's lifestyle. If your Pug plays and walks in wooded areas, you may want to ask your vet about vaccines for tick-borne illnesses, like Lyme disease. Show Pugs, or Pugs that frequently are housed in kennels, may be recommended to receive vaccines against Bordetella (also called kennel cough) or coronavirus.

Common Ailments of the Pug

The unique Pug anatomy does make them susceptible to a number of ailments. Many of these are linked to their genes, meaning you can often tell if your Pug is prone to them by looking at their parents.

Eye problems

Pug eyes are large and pronounced. This makes them more prone to injury. Pugs are also known to exhibit a number of genetic eye diseases. These include:

- **Keratoconjunctivitis sicca.** Also called "dry cyc," this is common in older Pugs. It occurs when not enough tears are produced naturally, leading to irritation and long-term eye damage if left untreated. It can be treated using medicated eye drops.
- **Pigmentary keratitis.** This is an inflammation of the cornea. You'll typically see a dark pigment spreading across the eye, which can lead to vision impairment if left untreated.

Orthopedic concerns

The sturdy build of the Pug means it's prone to some joint and bone problems that are more often seen in larger breeds. Many of these are hereditary, so you can determine the likelihood of your Pug developing these problems by looking at their lineage. Your

Pug may be suffering from joint problems if he moves stiffly or is reluctant to move.

The most common orthopedic problems seen in Pugs are:

- **Patellar luxation.** Also called "slipped stifle," this is a dislocation of the kneecaps due to weak or misaligned tendons. Afflicted Pugs normally have a variant called medial luxation, where the knee drifts outward. You may see your Pug hopping instead of walking, or having difficulty straightening his legs.

- **Hip dysplasia.** Common in large dogs, this occurs when the hip bone won't fit correctly in the joint. It can lead to impaired movement and severe pain and is most common in obese Pugs. While serious cases require surgery, it can often be treated with physical therapy and anti-inflammatory medication.

- **Legg-Calve-Perthes disease.** This is a condition in which the blood supply is impaired to the ball of the hip. The joint gradually weakens, causing permanent lameness. This condition typically manifests in puppies between 4 and 10 months old. It may require surgery for treatment, depending on the severity.

Respiratory ailments

Short-faced dogs like Pugs often have more difficulty breathing, especially in humid or hot weather. Some Pugs have deformities in the bones of the face that add to these problems. If this is the case, the problem will only get worse as the Pug ages, so it's best to have it surgically corrected as soon as it's detected.

These breathing problems in Pugs are referred to collectively as brachycephalic syndrome and are one of the more costly Pug ailments to correct. The surgery typically costs $800-$1,000 (£600-£770). Two specific conditions are typically the cause of the problem:

- **Stenotic nares.** The nares are the nasal passages, and stenotic means constricted or narrow. Basically, this means your Pug's nostrils are too small, forcing him to breathe through his mouth and work harder for air. Pugs with this condition are especially loud snorers and can be noisy breathers, especially after exercise. If your Pug has this condition, a harness is much better than a collar. You should also be especially mindful of obesity, and not let him exert himself in warm weather, as these can make the condition worse.

- **Elongated soft palate.** The soft palate is the top part of the mouth. When it's too long, the airways become blocked, leading to loud snorting and snoring. Uncorrected, it can put a lot of strain on your Pug's lungs and heart, reducing his lifespan.

Skin problems

A Pug's wrinkly skin can trap moisture, and that leads to the growth of bacteria. This makes Pugs susceptible to a number of skin diseases. Symptoms common to all of them are scratching, chewing, or licking, but there are also specific signs that can help you identify a skin infection from chewing caused by allergies or parasites.

Specific skin ailments include:

- **Hot Spots**. Also known as "acute moist dermatitis," these are red, oozing areas on your dog's skin. They'll often be warm and moist, as well, and typically are found on the lower back and insides of the legs. They're a common secondary infection for Pugs with fleas or mites, especially in hot weather.

- **Pyodermas**. These bacterial infections can be thought of as a form of canine acne. You'll see red bumps or blackheads on the face, genitals, or skin folds. Most of the time, it clears up on its own, but in severe cases, a vet can prescribe medicated shampoos for treatment.

- **Yeast infections**. Some yeast occurs naturally on the skin of a Pug. If there's too much, though, it causes a skin infection known as Malassezia dermatitis. The signs include greasy skin or thickened skin with an increase in pigmentation. It's most often seen on the face, in the ears, and between the toes.

Other Hereditary Diseases:

- **Pug-dog encephalitis**. This disease causes inflammation of the brain. While it's believed to be hereditary, unfortunately, little is known about it. There is no treatment and no test for predisposition. Affected Pugs are lethargic and often stagger or walk in circles. They may also have vision problems, seizures, or press their heads against surfaces. It typically presents in Pugs two years or younger, and is quickly fatal.

- **Epilepsy**. This brain disorder may be hereditary and is one of the most common canine neurological disorders. Pugs are prone to epilepsy, and there is no screening test currently available. Typically you won't see signs until the Pug is an adult, and it will manifest as seizures that usually last anywhere from a few seconds to several minutes. Epilepsy can't be cured, but it can be treated and controlled with medication.

Preventing Obesity

Obesity is a common problem for Pugs. They like food and aren't especially active, and that can be a dangerous combination. The best way to prevent obesity in your Pug is to make sure he's getting his daily walk and to carefully monitor his food intake.

If there are multiple people caring for the Pug, make sure he's not getting duplicate treats or meals. If you have cats or other animals, you'll need to make sure he doesn't have access to their food, too. Pugs are one breed you can't trust to self-regulate their food intake. Most of them will eat pretty much anything that's available.

A general rule of thumb is that you should be able to feel your Pug's ribs through his skin but shouldn't be able to see them. Even a stocky dog like the Pug should have a visible waist when viewed from above. Other signs of obesity include difficulty jumping onto furniture and a waddling gait.

If you suspect you have a chubby Pug, ask your vet for their recommendation of the best dog food for overweight Pugs. You may want to reduce the amount you're feeding, reduce the caloric content of the food, or both. Increasing the amount of fiber in your Pug's diet can also help. Incorporate freshly cooked vegetables like carrots or green beans into their food. This will help them feel full without adding a lot of calories.

Can a Pug Develop Allergies?

Allergies are relatively rare in Pugs, but they do happen. Some Pugs are allergic to certain foods, while others develop allergies to environmental factors like mold or pollen. Allergies are, unfortunately, difficult to diagnose. The main symptoms tend to be itchy skin and ears, changes in the coat, and dry or flaking patches on the skin. Your best bet if you notice these symptoms is to contact your vet. Together, you can develop a plan to identify and treat the allergy.

Some allergies are inherited, and others are developed. Inherited allergies are known as Allergic skin disease, and will typically show up in the Pug's early adulthood (around one to three years old).

If you see an allergic reaction in your Pug, identify any recent changes in his environment or diet. Limit his exposure to these potential sources one by one until you've found the cause. Avoidance is the best Pug allergy treatment, though in severe cases, your vet can prescribe medication.

Food allergies

The most common food allergens for Pugs are corn and wheat. You'll normally see red bumps on his skin, often on the feet, ears, or stomach. To identify the allergen, your vet will likely suggest switching your Pug to a hypoallergenic diet for a few weeks to see if the symptoms clear. At this point, you can re-introduce potential allergens until you've found the culprit.

Environmental allergens

The two most environmental sources of allergies in Pugs are:

- **Atopy.** An allergy to pollen or grass, this is a seasonal affliction, similar to pollen allergies in people. Your Pug will constantly scratch at his ears and face during high-pollen times. Secondary infections are common, as well, especially bacterial ear infections.
- **Flea allergy dermatitis.** Some Pugs are especially sensitive to flea saliva. You'll see raised, red, bumpy patches on the skin around where he was bitten by fleas. The reaction will clear as soon as you can get rid of the fleas.

Common Pug Parasites

Even an indoor Pug can pick up parasites. These small critters can either be on your dog (external parasites, like fleas, mites, and ticks) or in your dog (internal parasites, like worms). In both cases, they can be very tricky to get rid of, so prevention is the ideal.

External parasites fall into three main categories:

- **Fleas.** Over 50% of skin problems in Pugs seen by vets are caused by fleas. Thankfully, flea control has gotten a lot easier over the years. You can get topical treatments, which you apply monthly to prevent eggs laid on your dog from hatching. Alternatively, you can get flea prevention tablets, which directly kill adults and sterilize females.

  If your Pug does get fleas, you can eradicate them using medicated shampoos. Don't forget to steam clean your furniture and carpets—flea eggs can survive a surprisingly long time in the right conditions.

- **Ticks.** Ticks aren't as pervasive as fleas, but they can be far more harmful. Ticks carry a variety of potentially fatal diseases, and the population has been steadily growing over the past few years. Check your Pug for ticks any time he's been in tall grass or a wooded area. If you find a tick, remove it immediately by grabbing the head with a pair of tweezers and pulling away with steady pressure.

  Finding a tick isn't an immediate emergency. Most tick-borne illnesses require several hours of contact to transfer. So even if the tick was infected, your dog might not be. Even so, it's a good idea to preserve the tick in a jar of rubbing alcohol for a week or two. If your Pug develops symptoms of an illness, the tick can help your vet diagnose and cure it.

- **Mites.** All dogs have a few mites living on them, just like people. The problem occurs when the population proliferates, often as a result of an impaired immune system. The four species most common in Pugs are Demodicosis (red mange), Scabies (sarcoptic mange), Cheyletiellosis (walking dandruff), and ear mites. All can be diagnosed by your vet using skin scrapings and treated with medicated shampoos.

The common internal parasites for Pugs are all different species of worm that live in the internal organs. The diagnosis is best achieved by checking the dog's poop. They'll also cause your dog's butt to itch, so he may scoot across the carpet. There are four main species of worm Pug owners should know about:

- **Roundworms.** This is the most common internal parasite across canine breeds. It occurs when the dog ingests infected dirt (or feces) and can be transmitted to humans. Roundworms are most concerning in puppies, causing vomiting and diarrhea. Many adult Pugs develop a resistance, but you can also get medications to prevent roundworm infection.

- **Hookworms.** Most common in the Southwest United States, hookworms enter the Pug's body like roundworms: through infected dirt or feces. They feed on your Pug's blood, which causes malnutrition and anemia. The main symptom is bloody diarrhea. While they can be fatal in the long-term, they can be prevented or treated with medication, and are rarely seen in adult Pugs.

- **Tapeworms.** These worms live in the intestines and feed on nutrients from what your Pug eats. They're transmitted to dogs by intermediary hosts, mostly external parasites like fleas or ticks. You can treat tapeworms with medication.

- **Heartworms.** The most serious internal parasites are heartworms. They're spread through mosquitos, making them very pervasive. They live inside the heart, are difficult to diagnose and treat, and can be fatal. Because of this, most vets will recommend a preventative heartworm treatment, starting at around 6-8 weeks old.

CHAPTER 14

Pug Grooming

The Pug is touted as a low-maintenance breed, and a lot of this has to do with how easy it is to groom. Pug grooming doesn't require you to get a set of trimming shears and certainly won't require a professional. Even in the show ring, you won't see a shaved Pug or one with extreme styling needs. Their laid-back temperament is reflected in their typical coat.

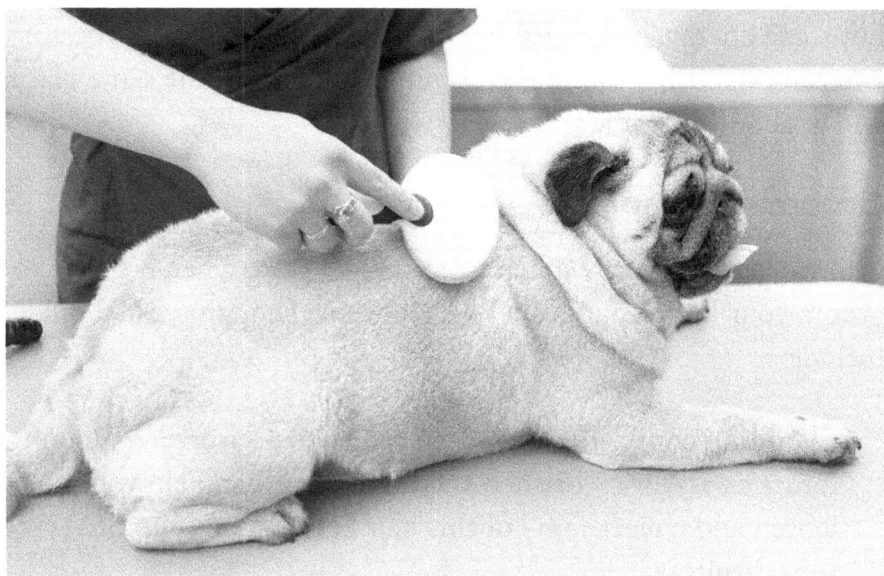

Regular brushing is the main part of your Pug's grooming routine.

Grooming your Pug involves more than just his hair and coat. Establishing a good grooming routine is important for your Pug's overall health, and it includes maintaining his teeth, wrinkles, and nails. Get your Pug used to being handled all over his body from the first day you bring him home. This includes opening his mouth to check his teeth, rubbing his belly, and handling his paws. If he gets accustomed to this when he's young, he'll be less resistant to grooming as he ages.

A grooming session is also a fantastic opportunity to bond with your new puppy. It's also the perfect opportunity to check your Pug for any health problems or parasites. You won't have to go through his full grooming routine until he's an adult. But start with weekly brushings and tooth cleanings as soon as you can.

Take your Pug out for a walk before you start grooming. This makes it less likely he'll pee on you, first of all, but can also get out some energy, so he's calmer while you're working. It's best if you can establish a routine, grooming your Pug in the same place and at about the same time every week.

Grooming supplies

You won't need to buy much from the pet store when it's time to groom your Pug. Your basic Pug grooming shopping list should include:

- **Shedding comb.** The hairy Pug can shed a surprising amount for its size. A wire-bristled shedding comb can help you loosen and collect some of this hair before it ends up on your furniture.

- **Bristle brush or brushing glove.** Along with the shedding comb, you'll want to have a soft Pug brush for daily coat maintenance. Shedding gloves can be great for Pugs since they feel just like being petted. Brushing helps stimulate the production of natural oils and distribute them across your Pug's coat. It also helps remove dead skin cells and hair.

- **Nail trimmer.** Both Dremel-style and plier-style trimmers can work for Pugs. Some Pugs are thrown off by the vibration of a Dremel tool; other owners swear by them since they're less likely to clip the quick of a squirmy Pug.

- **Styptic powder.** Just in case you do nick the quick during nail care, it's good to have styptic powder on hand to stop the bleeding and prevent infection.

- **Dog toothbrush and toothpaste.** You should use a dog-specific toothpaste. Human toothpaste contains chemicals that could hurt a Pug if swallowed. Dog toothpaste is also flavored like meat or peanut butter—things your Pug will want in his mouth. A fingertip toothbrush is often the easiest style to use in the small mouth of a Pug.

- **Dog shampoo.** Again, don't just use your human shampoo. A dog's fur has different needs, and shampoos made for people can strip the essential oils from their fur, leading to dry skin and allergies. Also, avoid chemical pest shampoos unless you're dealing with an active infestation. If you want to add an extra layer of protection, consider a shampoo with a natural insecticide like tea tree oil or citronella.

- **Q-tips or cotton balls.** These are the best tools for cleaning out Pug wrinkles

How Often Do Pugs Shed Hair?

It depends on the Pug. Like other dogs with two coats, Pugs naturally shed seasonally: in fall, when their winter coat comes in, and in spring, when their winter coat is dropped. Pugs that spend the majority of their time in a temperature-controlled environment may not follow this pattern, however. Indoor Pugs often shed at a consistent level year-round.

Pay attention to the hair level in your home so you can get ahead of seasonal shedding. For seasonal shedders, you'll probably want to brush them daily during their shed period. This will prevent much of the hair from reaching your furniture. For year-round shedders, brush them weekly with the wide side of a metal comb to free loose hair and debris.

Bathing

Most Pugs only need a path every few months. They're not known for developing bad body odor, and their close coat doesn't tangle readily or attract much debris. It all depends on your Pug, of course, and how dirty he likes to get on a regular basis.

A Pug bath can easily take place in most kitchen sinks. A lot of owners find this easier than filling up the bathtub. Put a no-skid surface on the bottom of the sink or tub first, so your Pug can stand up comfortably during his bath time.

Start by brushing your Pug to remove any loose hair or trapped debris. Once this is done, transfer your Pug to the empty sink or tub and pour warm water over him, starting with the head and working back toward the tail. Use your hand as a shield to keep the water from getting in his eyes when you pour it on his head.

Once your Pug is wet all over, lather him up with dog shampoo. Again, start at the neck and work back. Don't use shampoo on his face. You don't want to risk getting it in your Pug's eyes— Pug eyes are very sensitive and prone to injury. Instead, use a clean, damp washcloth to wipe his face and wrinkles.

After lathering, rinse the shampoo off with clean, warm water. Make sure you get all the shampoo rinsed away; residue left behind can make your dog itchy and make his coat look dull. Towel-dry your Pug as much as you can before you take him out of the sink. He'll want to shake once you take him out, and towel-drying reduces the mess. From this point, you can let him air dry or use a blow dryer on its lowest setting if you want to speed up the process.

Caring for Pug Wrinkles

Moisture can become trapped in the wrinkles on a Pug's face, and this makes the perfect conditions for fungus and bacteria to grow. To prevent this, you'll want to clean your Pug's wrinkles once a week. Use a dampened Q-Tip or cotton ball to gently wipe between each wrinkle, then thoroughly dry with a towel. Usually, this is easier if you sit behind the Pug and clean from above—many Pugs get uncomfortable with their faces being touched from the front.

Pug Eye and Ear Care

You want to check your Pug's eyes and ears once a week. If your puppy has a parasite infection, illness, or other ailments, the eyes and ears are where you'll likely see the first sign. Check the ears for waxy build-up. A small amount of ear wax is normal, but

you should clean them if the ears look crusted up. Use a cotton ball dampened with ear cleaner and gently wipe in an outwards motion, so you don't push the wax further into the ear canal.
If the ear looks red or swollen, has a dark-colored build-up, or smells bad, contact your vet—your Pug may have ear mites or an ear infection.

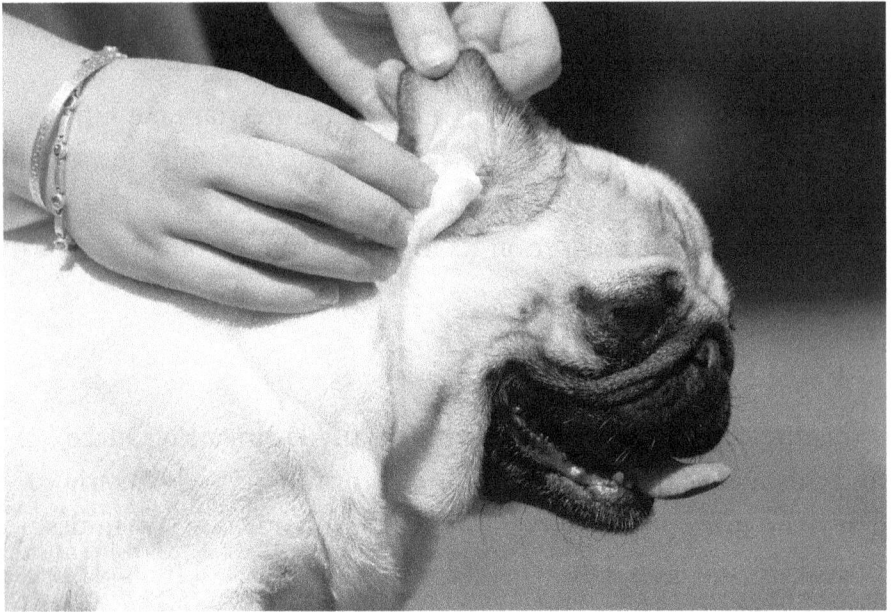

Keeping your Pug's ears clean will help prevent infection and parasites.

Look around your Pug's eyes for signs of irritation. Some Pugs need their eyes wiped daily with a damp cloth to clear small amounts of discharge. This is normal, but if you see oozing or substantial discharge, you should contact your vet, especially if the Pug's eyes are red or hazy.

Pug Dental Care

Pugs are more prone to dental problems than other breeds because of their underbite and small mouth. This makes it especially important to brush their teeth at least once a week— and once a day is better if you have the time for it.

Start your brushing in the front of the mouth and work backward, doing the upper teeth first, followed by the lower. Make sure you're getting into all the crevices by the gum line, where plaque is most likely to accumulate and lead to gum diseases.

A baby Pug dog will probably take a little while to get used to a human finger in his mouth. The more experience he has with tooth brushing, though, the more normal it will be for him.

Pug Nail Care

Trimming your Pug's nails is likely to be the most difficult part of his regular grooming, and is the thing most Pug owners (and dog owners in general) dread doing the most. Pugs don't like being forced to sit still, and they're often very squirmy during nail trimming sessions. Because of this, you may want to have two people on-hand, despite the Pug's small size.

Most Pugs need their nails trimmed monthly. You can tell it's time for trimming if you hear your dog's nails when he's walking on a hard surface. And trimming is necessary, especially for mostly-indoor breeds like the Pug. Left too long, your dog's nails can curl in toward the pad of the foot, making it painful to walk.

Dog nails have a vein in the center, known as the quick. This is where the only nerves in the nail are located, so you want to avoid cutting the quick when you're trimming. If you do hit the quick, it will bleed, and your Pug will likely whimper in pain.

Some Pugs have dark nails, while others are lighter. In lighter nails, you'll be able to see the quick running down the center. In a darker nail, you can tell where it starts by looking for the place the nail starts to curve.

Trim a little at a time so you can prevent hitting this sensitive area. Start with one of the front paws, and work a paw at a time. If you do hit the quick, apply a bit of styptic powder to stop the bleeding and cut less from the next nail. Make sure you give your Pug a treat and lots of praise at the end of every session—even if it's not painful, Pugs don't enjoy the tedium of a nail clipping session.

CHAPTER 15

Pug Shows and Competitions

The Pug is a natural performer, and this makes it well-suited to shows, competitions, or anywhere else it can be the center of attention. And Pugs do well overall in the show ring. The Pug has won Best in Show at the Westminster Dog Show, though it's been a little while (the Pug Dhandy's Favorite Woodchuck was the 1981 winner). When it comes to Best in Group, Pugs are more successful. The most recent group champion Pug, Westminster Dog Show 2018 Toy Group winner, was Biggie the Pug. Pugs have won the Toy Group at Westminster a total of 9 times.

The Pug dog price will likely go up if he's the offspring of an AKC champion.

A Pug dog show isn't just about conformation, either. These active little comedians can do well on the agility course, and they excel in the freestyle ring. Training for these events can be a lot of fun for both you and your dog.

Showing an animal can be a lot of work—and not every Pug will take to it. You'll also end up spending a lot of money on training, grooming, and travel. Keeping a show dog can be a big-time commitment, too, especially if you want to be competitive on the national level.

The best way to figure out if showing your Pug is a good idea is to go to a local Pug Show. These smaller events will give you a chance to meet the breeders and talk to them about what all is involved.

Classification

The American Kennel Club classifies the Pug as a member of the Toy group. This puts it in competition with breeds like the Shi Tzu, Toy Poodle, and Chihuahua. If you're not a big fan of small dogs in general, that's something you'll want to keep in mind—you'll be seeing a lot of them at shows. Both the UK Kennel Club and the CKC also classify the Pug in the Toy group.

Finding AKC Pug Puppies

Conformation is the event you think of when you picture a dog show. It isn't just about finding the prettiest dog. Judges are looking for the dog that is the best representative of its breed, as expressed in the AKC Pug standard. If you're interested in showing Pugs, you should review this breed standard before you start shopping for your puppies.

Much of the AKC standard concerns the physical appearance of the Pug. It should have a strong, sturdy body with a well-rounded head. Fawn Pugs must have a black facial mask, and a thumbprint on the forehead is ideal. There are standards for everything from the lay of the tail to the shape of the ears. You may want to go through it with a breeder so they can explain the different terms and tell you what to look for.

There is also a component of the AKC Pug standard related to temperament. More than other breeds, Pugs tend to be showmen in the ring—and this charisma is something the judges look for. An outgoing, playful Pug is going to be the best suited to conformation.

All puppies registered with the AKC have to have a pedigree that verifies they are purebred Pugs. This means you have to buy your puppy from a breeder. AKC Pug puppies for sale will often cost more than puppies bred as family pets, especially if they come from a championship lineage.

Breeders of AKC Pug puppies also tend to be more selective about who they'll sell to, especially the puppies they think have the most competitive potential. They may put extra clauses in their contract, as well, for example, about who gets the puppies if you should choose to breed. Most breeders won't sell a potential champion to someone with no experience in the show ring, so you may need to start small and work your way up.

Faults of the Pug breed

Faults are physical traits that either lower a Pug's score or disqualify it from conformation altogether. Obviously, you'll want to avoid these if you can when you're shopping for AKC Pugs for sale. Keep in mind that some faults will not be visible until the Pug is over 6 months old. Look at the Pug's lineage to see if any faults were present in previous generations.

There are two types of faults. Structural faults involve the Pug's body structure and movement. Common structural faults of the Pug are especially long or short legs, legs that don't turn in, or a lean or long body.

There are also cosmetic faults that relate only to the Pug's appearance. These include Pugs that are "mitted," with lighter fur on their paws. A wooly coat is another cosmetic fault. Many cosmetic faults relate to the face, like a wry mouth, an overbite, or a long muzzle.

Some faults are more serious than others, and a Pug with minor faults can still enjoy the competition ring. Most faults won't affect a Pug's health in any way, either. Even a Pug with major physical faults can still be a happy, wonderful family pet—they're just not the best choice for the show ring.

Acceptable coat colors

The AKC is the most limiting when it comes to acceptable Pug colors. Only fawn and black Pugs are allowed to enter conformation. Having said that, apricot and silver Pugs whose coloration is close enough to fawn may be registered as such for competition. Other coat colors, including an albino Pug or true brindle Pug, are considered to be disqualifications.

Other kennel clubs have slightly broader definitions of acceptable coats. Both the UK Kennel Club and the CKC will accept fawn Pugs, black Pugs, apricot Pugs, and silver Pugs. Just like the AKC, though, all-white Pugs and multi-hued Pugs, including merle and brindle coats, are disqualified.

Grooming to the AKC Pug Standard

The Pug is one of the easiest dogs to breed to the AKC standard. You can trim the stray hairs on their legs or body to give the Pug a cleaner look, but often the only preparation he needs is a quick bath. You should bathe your Pug a couple days before the show. Doing it too soon before can give the coat a fluffy feel that judges won't like.

Other Competitive Events

Pugs aren't especially athletic, but they're a very adaptable breed, and this makes them perfect for skill competitions. Events like agility and freestyle can also be a better choice for the independent Pug, especially if you have a particularly active and energetic animal.

Pugs can really enjoy learning to run agility courses.

The rules for other events are often less restrictive than those for Conformation. Physical faults aren't considered, and in most cases, you can compete with dogs that have been spayed and neutered. This can make these events great if you want to dip your toe in competitive waters with your family pet, rather than shopping specifically for a show dog.

You can find specialized training courses for all the events below through the AKC and Pug breed clubs. Each of the sports has its own clubs, too, who can give you more information. Check with them to find out how you can get your Pug involved.

Obedience

Pugs admittedly aren't the most common breed to see in obedience contests. Their stubbornness and independence can be detriments in this kind of competition. Having said that, Pugs are also very intelligent, and select individuals have earned advanced obedience titles.

If your Pug takes readily to learning new commands, obedience might be a good fit for him. Pugs with a calmer, more laid-back temperament are also more likely to excel in this event than a very excitable or rambunctious Pug.

Agility

Agility is a competitive obstacle course for dogs, where animals from various breeds compete against each other to get the fastest time and the cleanest run. Dogs are judged not only on how quickly they complete obstacles but how accurate they are in doing so, giving shorter-legged breeds a fighting chance to compete.

It's pretty fun to watch a Pug racing over an agility course. What this smart dog lacks in speed it makes up for accuracy. Energetic Pugs make the best candidates for agility. While a dog can compete as young as 6 months old, make sure your Pug has mastered his basic commands and obedience before starting in on this more advanced training.

Freestyle

While not as well-known as obedience or agility, freestyle is an event every Pug owner should know about. It might as well have been made for this comic of the dog world. Freestyle involves the dog and its handler performing a routine set to music, often while wearing thematic costumes. The contents of the routine can be a mix of dancing, tricks, and obedience exercises, making it in some ways a combination of the two events above.

The Pug's personality makes them excellent competitors in musical freestyle. They're good at learning tricks and routines, and they love to perform. There is another form of freestyle, called Heelwork, that is closer to obedience in that it involves heeling the dog on various sides. Heelwork can be a bit more frustrating to work on with a Pug, but they do tend to do well with the routines.

CHAPTER 16

Pugs as Working Dogs

T he Pug was bred as a companion, but that's not all they can do. While you'll never see a Pug herding or hunting, this lovable breed has other important working functions—including some in the medical field.

The Pug's playful disposition makes it perfect for therapy work.

The main working function of the Pug is as a service animal. Pug service dogs can be hearing dogs for the deaf, therapy dogs for nursing homes or hospitals, and emotional support dogs for both children and adults. Many of the same things that make them ideal family pets are key to their work in this area.

Pug Service Dogs

Pugs are smart, alert, and friendly with strangers. They're easy to train, easy to groom, and sturdy enough to withstand frequent handling. All-told, this describes the ideal therapy dog. Patients visited by therapy dogs are shown to have reduced blood pressure and lower instances of depression, one of the reasons many institutions have taken to employing these adorable helpers.

The official name for therapy dogs is Animal Assisted Therapy. While the training for this kind of work is less intensive than for seeing-eye dogs, not just any Pug can jump into the position. The ideal Pug therapy dog is well-socialized to a wide array of different stimuli. There's a lot of equipment in a hospital that will be unusual for most dogs, including crutches and walkers that can catch a stray paw. Before a Pug can become a service dog, their basic obedience skills have to be on-point.

Becoming A Therapy Dog

There are several organizations you can reach out to if you're interested in certifying your Pug as a therapy dog.

- **Love on a Leash.** This non-profit volunteer organization was founded in the 1980s to bring therapy animals to facilities in southern California. Since then, they've grown to include over 2,000 members across the United States. You can find all the information you need to join on their website (http://www.loveonaleash.org).

- **Pet Partners.** Formerly known as the Delta Society, they were the first group formed to promote therapy animals, founded in 1977. They provide therapy animals for a wide range of patients, including veterans with PTSD, those with learning disabilities, and seniors with Alzheimer's. They have a presence in both the United States and Canada if you're looking to get involved. Their website (http://www.petpartners.org) has information on signing up, as well as educational resources.

- **Therapy Dog International.** The widest-reaching of the groups listed, Therapy Dog International, was founded in the mid-'70s and today has more than 20,000 registered dogs on its roster. Information on volunteering or signing your dog up can be found at http://www.tdi-dog.org.

Other Working Functions

Pugs are a bit too affectionate with strangers to work well as a guard dog. They can make excellent alert dogs, however. They can be trained easily to bark on command in response to certain stimuli—one reason they're sometimes used as hearing dogs.

As you saw from the famous Pugs listed in Chapter 2, there are plenty of Pugs working in Hollywood, as well. This photogenic breed is a favorite for the silver screen. Famous Pugs who were actors include:

- Harley the Pug (Patrick Pug in the 2018 movie)
- Mushu the Pug (Frank in *Men in Black* and *Men in Black II*)

- Cheeka (famous for Hutch Cellular commercials in India)

If you think your Pug would enjoy being an actor or model, start by reaching out to a local Pug club. The members may have experience that will help you get started.

CHAPTER 17

Breeding Pugs

Breeding any animal is a serious responsibility, and not one that should be undertaken lightly. To be a responsible breeder, you need to be able to properly care for both the parents and the puppies at every stage of their lives. You also need to have a basic understanding of genetics and common breeding practices, so you know what you're looking for in a mated pair.

When seeking out a female Pug for sale for breeding,
pay attention to both her health and temperament.

Don't start breeding because you think it's a quick, easy way to make some money. While purebred Pugs can fetch a high price, establishing a breeding program can take some serious investment money. It will likely take a couple years until you start turning a profit (if you ever do). And breeding is a lot of work, too. Between caring for the parents and raising newborn baby Pugs, running a quality breeding program can, at times, be a full-time job. If you decide to breed, do it because you love Pugs, not because you want to make money.

You should have a lot of experience with Pugs before you start breeding them. As a breed, they have some very unique requirements and traits. If you've never owned a Pug before, spend at least a couple years with a pet Pug, getting comfortable with the breed, before you start to breed.

Many breeders also show their dogs, and this is something you should consider. People will pay more for the offspring of a championship Pug, for one thing. It's also a great way to get more familiar with the breed and its standards.

If you're serious about breeding, your education should involve more than buying some Pug books. Ask local breeders if they have any tips. Find out how they got started, and take any advice they give you to heart. Breeding newborn Pug puppies can be very rewarding, but it's also a big responsibility—one you should be absolutely sure you're ready for before you get started.

Should You Breed Your Pug?

Along with figuring out if you, as the owner, are ready to breed, you should make sure it's a good idea for your Pug. When it comes to female Pugs, most of them are actually not especially good mothers. They're often less devoted to their puppies than other breeds, leaving you responsible more often for the newborn Pug's care.

If your female Pug is especially aloof and stubborn with people, it's more likely she'll have that attitude with her puppies. This isn't necessarily a reason not to breed her, as long as you're prepared to do a bit of extra work.

The most important thing is that both parents are healthy. This is especially important for the female. She should be in top form and getting the ideal nutrition well before you decide to breed. Pregnancy takes a lot out of a dog's body, so failing to take the mother's health into account can be a danger to both her and her baby Pug puppies.

Signs not to breed

Deciding whether you should breed a Pug is definitely a dog-by-dog decision. Having said that, there are some red flags across the board. Generally speaking, you don't want to breed a dog that has traits that shouldn't exist in the Pug line. The biggest red flags include:

- **Hereditary diseases.** If your Pug has a genetic disorder, including eye problems, joint problems, or idiopathic epilepsy, you should not breed them. Carriers of these diseases may be bred if they have other traits that are especially desirable, but you should avoid breeding them with another carrier of that disorder.

- **Temperament problems.** Don't breed any Pug that shows extreme behavior, whether that's aggressiveness and biting or introversion and shyness. These temperament issues can be passed down the line, and they're not something you want to perpetuate.

- **Red Mange (Demodicosis).** The mites that cause Red Mange are present on most animals. An excess of these mites, or sensitivity to them, may be hereditary, however. To be safe, you shouldn't breed any animal that's had this issue.

- **Bilateral or unilateral cryptorchidism.** Specific to male dogs, this is a condition where one or both testicles don't descend. Dogs with bilateral cryptorchidism are sterile and can't be bred. Even in unilateral cryptorchidism, though, the dogs have a higher instance of testicular cancer and may experience other health issues.

Finding a Mate

Ideal breeding isn't just about picking two exceptional animals and putting them together. You want to pick traits that complement each other, filling in one parent's weaknesses with the other parent's strengths.

This is where knowledge of genetics really comes into play. While you don't necessarily need to be able to read a canine genome to be a successful breeder, you should understand the way dominant and recessive traits interact, and how selective breeding can be used to emphasize certain traits over others.

Keep in mind that you can't control how the genes interact. You should be aware of all the traits each dog exhibits, and think about what will happen in the "worst-case scenario"—in other words, if the exact traits you're hoping will stay recessive come out. Compare both parents with a mind toward what problems could arise, too. Don't let yourself be blinded to potential issues because of how appealing the dogs' good traits are.

Buying vs. Studding

Many breeders only own a female Pug and find a male Pug to pair with her. This practice is known as studding. You may have to pay a monetary stud fee, while other owners of male Pugs ask for a portion of the resulting litter in payment. If you already have an unneutered male Pug you want to breed, your best bet is to look for female Pugs for sale that will complement his traits.

Keep in mind that you want to control when your Pugs breed. If you have an un-spayed female and an unneutered male living in the same house, they should have separate pens and living spaces when you're not actively breeding them. This will prevent any unexpected pregnancies and accidental over-breeding. The need for two separate Pug spaces is the main reason many breeders prefer studding.

Studding is recommended for beginning breeders. You'll have enough stress paying attention to the puppies once they are born without worrying about taking care of both parents. Studding also gives you the chance to introduce more genetic variety into your line. Once your kennel is established, and you have more experience, you can decide whether it's time to keep multiple breeding animals on-site.

Common breeding techniques

There are a lot of different breeding approaches out there, and most breeders will tell you there are pros and cons to every strategy. You should discuss this with other breeders you know before you make your decision, but just to get you started, here are some terms and concepts you should know about. Most breeders will use a combination of different breeding techniques, at different points in their breeding process, to fine-tune and perfect their line.

- **Inbreeding.** There's a certain stigma to this word for many people, but when it comes to dogs, inbreeding can be a legitimate practice. It is the practice of breeding closely related dogs together, such as siblings or a parent with its child. Inbreeding is useful for emphasizing existing traits in a breeding line. Make sure the dogs have few to no defects. Both positive and negative traits are intensified by in-breeding, so it's especially important to be intimately familiar with the pedigree of your line before beginning.

- **Outcrossing.** The opposite of inbreeding, outcrossing is the breeding of completely unrelated dogs. You can use this to introduce a new trait into your line. It's also helpful in correcting existing faults in the line, and can generally help to keep Pug puppies healthy and vibrant by preserving genetic diversity. The disadvantage of outcrossing is that it can introduce unexpected traits, or bring out previously recessive traits you hadn't been aware of.

- **Line-breeding.** Similar to inbreeding, this involves breeding animals that are related but with a further degree of separation—for example, breeding cousins, or a grandsire with a younger dame. Line-breeding intensifies both positive and negative traits, but to a lesser degree than inbreeding.

Pug Pregnancy

Pug pregnancy is very fast compared to a human's. It lasts from 60-65 days or 8-9 weeks. A female Pug starts showing signs of pregnancy around the second to third week. You'll notice she's a bit lethargic, and she may clean herself more often. Her stomach may also start to swell, and she may have slight nausea in the morning and a decreased appetite. As soon as you suspect your Pug is pregnant, you should set up a vet appointment to confirm it and find out how far along she is.

Dietary supplements aren't recommended for most Pugs, but you can ask your vet to make sure. Don't give any supplements or vitamins without consulting your vet. They can accumulate in your Pug's blood and tissue, actually causing harm to the developing baby Pugs. Too much calcium is especially problematic, potentially causing a life-threatening condition in puppies.

Signs of pregnancy are very clear by the fourth week. Physically, she'll have a distended stomach, and her appetite will pick back up— she may eat twice as much as she did before, and will need more protein in her diet. Don't worry about limiting her diet. She needs a lot of calories, so you should feed her whenever she's hungry.

She'll also start to nest around the fourth week as she prepares for the birth. Don't be surprised if any towels, sweaters, and other soft things lying around are dragged into your Pug's dog bed. If she normally sleeps in bed with you, you'll probably need to set your Pug up her own place to sleep. She might also have difficulty going up stairs or getting onto furniture, so keep an eye on your Pug and make adjustments as necessary.

By the fifth week, your Pug will be very easily tired, and will probably want to stay at home most of the time. You may want to get a place for her to pee inside, so she doesn't need to take as many walks. She'll also be less sociable—if there are other animals in the house, you may want to isolate her from them. If you have the male Pug in the house, isolate him from the dame at this point, too, and keep him away until the puppies are at least 4 weeks old.

At around 6 weeks, you can have an X-ray taken to tell you how many puppies there will be. This is recommended so you can make sure all of the puppies are born—an unborn fetus left inside the mother can cause serious health complications.

If your Pug hasn't given birth by day 67 of her pregnancy, contact your vet. She may need assistance with delivering. Because the Pug's head is so large compared to its body, some Pugs have to be delivered by cesarean section. The X-ray at 6 weeks can also help your vet predict if natural birth will be an issue.

In most cases, it will be safe for your Pug to give birth at home. Discuss your plan with your vet. If you plan to take your Pug in for the delivery, make sure you know who to call when the office is closed—the baby Pugs might not wait until normal office hours to come. When your Pug's temperature drops under 100°F (38C), she'll give birth within the next 24 hours.

For a home birth, create your Pug a whelping box. Put a dog bed inside a cardboard box that has one side cut out of it. Layer plastic and newspaper on the bottom of the whelping box, so you can remove it as it gets soiled during the birth. Assemble all the supplies you'll need around the sixth week, just in case. These include clean towels, sterile thread, a thermometer, a disinfectant spray, a dropper, and a heating pad.

During labor, offer your Pug water, but not food—she'll likely throw it up if she does eat. She'll likely whimper, pant, or shiver. Labor can last anywhere from 2-12 hours. The puppies can come quickly, or there can be an hour or two between them. Don't try to force the issue or intervene unless you see a true need. If a puppy becomes wedged, or if more than 2 hours pass between puppies, call your vet for assistance.

Most dames will bite their own umbilical cord. If yours doesn't, break it gently using sterilized thread. Your Pug will clean her puppies and push out the placenta. At this point, you can clean up the area. Keep a close eye on the puppies to make sure they're breathing and nursing. Don't move the puppies unless the mom seems aggressive toward them.

A Pug mother nurses her litter.

Caring for Newborn Baby Pugs

Most new Pug mothers will spend all their time with their puppies. You might even have some trouble getting her to go outside to the bathroom. Check on the puppies every few hours, especially if the Pug is a new mother. Make sure they're all warm and suckling. If any puppies are crying or cold, place them close to the mother, and watch to make sure they're not being pushed out by the other members of the litter. The nipples near the hind legs give the most milk, so if you have a runt or weak puppy, encourage them toward the mother's back end.

Your vet should examine the new puppies within 48 hours of birth. They'll check to make sure the milk is being produced and that there aren't any infections or other problems. They can also check the puppies for birth defects or issues.

In most cases, the mother Pug will see to it that the puppies are fed and kept warm for the first few weeks. If the mother refuses to stay with her puppies or doesn't seem interested in them, you may need to take a more active role. Warmth is important—puppies can't regulate their own body temperature until they're around 3 weeks old. Talk to your vet about setting up a warm space for them. You'll also need to feed them by hand using an eye-dropper. Don't resort to these measures unless absolutely necessary, however. The bonding time between a mommy Pug and her newborn puppies is important for their eventual socialization.

CHAPTER 18

Pug Mixes and Cross-Breeds

Purebred pugs are a delight, and the same qualities that make them such excellent pets are appealing for breeders of mixes and crosses. The pug's compact size, friendly temperament, and longevity are all attractive qualities the breed can bring to a pairing. You can't take a Pug mix to the show ring—but they often make very family companions. In some cases, you may find a Pug cross an even better match for your family. They're often less expensive than full breed Pug puppies, for one thing. They may also have fewer health concerns than either of their purebred parents.

Every animal is different. That's especially true when it comes to cross-breeds. While it's harder to establish a consistent profile, they do still have some typical traits. Let's look at some of the most popular Pug crosses.

The Puggle is just one of the adorable Pug cross-breeds you'll find.

The Pug Tzu

The Shih Tzu/Pug mix, known as the Pug Tzu, is an adorable toy dog that often brings out the best of these two beloved breeds. They tend to be lively and good-natured and get along well with both kids and other animals.

Compared to Pugs, Shih Tzu/Pug puppies require more attention and grooming time and are generally more active. They're also less resistant to heat—you may want to get a different breed if you live in a warmer climate.

The Puggle

The Puggle is half Pug, half Beagle. This Pug/Beagle cross has the wrinkled face of a Pug, but on a longer, taller body that makes them look a bit like miniature Mastiffs. Their temperament is gentle and fun-loving. Like Pugs, they're smart but stubborn—easy to train if you know the right treats to tempt them.

Puggles are equally adapted to be apartment-dwellers or country dogs. Keep in mind they're not quiet dogs. Puggles love to bark, especially as puppies, and they may howl as well in tribute to their Beagle lineage.

The Pugapoo

A cross of a Pug and a Poodle, the Pugapoo is a people-loving and very trainable puppy. Crossing with the Poodle may make this mixed Pug hypoallergenic, though you shouldn't count on this—as, with all mixed-breed traits, it can be unpredictable. The Pugapoo's coat can also vary widely, from the short coat of the Pug to the curly coat of the Poodle, and they range in size from 10 to 30 pounds (4.5 to 13.5 kilograms). They do tend to be excellent family dogs, a trait they get from both sides of their lineage.

Pug/Terrier Crosses

The Pug/Terrier mix is a popular combination. These dogs tend to be rambunctious, curious, and intelligent. They may also be stubborn or territorial, depending on the personality of the parents. Like Pugs and Terriers, they're prone to separation anxiety and can be noisy, especially as puppies.

Notable mixes include the Jug, a Jack Russell/Pug cross, the Pugshire, which crosses the Pug and the Yorkshire Terrier, and the Bugg, a mix of the Pug and the Boston Terrier. Both of these breeds are typically very affectionate lap dogs, loyal to their owners and small enough to live comfortably in apartments.

Miniature Pugs

Micro Pug, Mini Pug, Teacup Pug—there are a lot of different names for a tiny Pug, and since the terminology isn't standardized, you don't always know what they mean. When you see teacup Pugs for sale, it isn't just a small Pug. It may be a cross-breed of a Pug with a smaller breed, such as the Chihuahua (a cross also known as the Chug), or it could be a dwarf Pug, selectively bred for the dwarfism trait, rather than being different Pug breeds.

Miniature Pug puppies often have more health problems and shorter lifespans than their full-sized counterparts. This is especially true if the teacup Pug puppies were selectively bred for dwarfism. Having said that, Chihuahuas are not as robust a breed as the Pug. Mini Pug puppies that are actually Chug cross-breeds may still be more prone to illness than a purebred.

While a toy dog Pug is a cute idea, you may want to think twice when you see miniature Pugs for sale. A reputable breeder will not select for dwarfism because of the associated health risks. If you're looking for a smaller dog, consider buying a different breed.

If you're looking for mini Pugs for sale, be careful you're going through a reputable breeder.

Other Pug Mixes

There are as many potential Pug crosses out there as there are other dog breeds. While it's impossible to list them all, here are some other Pug cross-breeds you might want to consider as family pets.

- **The Bull Pug.** An English Bulldog/Pug mix, Bull Pugs are stocky, medium-sized dogs. Bull Pug puppies are affectionate and energetic, but as they age, Bull Pugs are a laid-back breed, less prone to separation anxiety than a purebred Pug.

- **The Cocker Pug.** A Pug/Cocker Spaniel cross, these dogs are loving, loyal, and friendly with both people and animals. Size-wise, they're slightly bigger than Pugs, with leaner legs. They're intelligent and eager to please, making them easy to train.

- **Corgi/Pug mix.** A cross-breed of a Pug and Corgi tends to be a stocky, muscular dog. They have a lot of energy and will need much more exercise than the typical Pug.

- **The Frug.** Also called a French Pug or a Frenchie Pug, this French Bulldog/Pug cross loves people and has a huge personality. They're a bit stockier than Pugs, and share the high intelligence of both their parent lines.

- **Pug/Golden Retriever mix.** These gentle dogs are easy to socialize with both people and other animals. They can also make good watchdogs since they're alert and quick to bark.

- **The Hug.** A Pug and Husky mix, the Hug typically can be thought of more as a small Husky than a variant of the Pug. They are very energetic and require lots of exercise.

- **Pug/Lab mix.** This is a relatively rare cross due to the differing sizes of the breeds. It is a beautiful animal, with the sleek body of a Labrador Retriever and the wrinkled face of a Pug. Their temperament tends to be gentle, sweet, and intelligent. They may acquire a stubborn streak from their Pug parents but are otherwise easy to train.

- **The Schnug.** A mini Schnauzer/Pug cross, the Schnug is notably smart and stubborn, even compared to Pugs. They're playful and active but enjoy a good cuddle too, making them a great family dog.

- **The Pug Shiba.** A Shiba Inu/Pug cross, these puppies tend to look like larger Pugs with less wrinkled faces. They're affectionate with their owners, though they can also be independent and aloof with strangers. Overall, they're less needy than a Pug, making them great for people who work during the day.

CHAPTER 19

Caring for an Aging Pug

Senior Pugs can be delightful home companions—more laid back than in their younger years, but just as loving and cuddly. Pug lovers have an advantage in this regard. Not only do Pugs tend to live longer than other breeds, they also are usually healthy for longer. Aside from more frequent vet visits, you might not notice any signs your Pug has reached his golden years until he's well past the decade mark.

Even with such hearty breeds, though, there are some things you should be aware of as your Pug ages. Knowing how to provide the right care for an old Pug will help you keep him healthy, happy, and comfortable as long as possible.

If you take care of him well, a senior Pug can still have a lot of happy years ahead of him.

When is a Pug Old?

The general rule of thumb for dogs is that they're seniors once they reach about 7 years old. This doesn't always seem to apply to the Pug, though, most of whom are still spry and active at this age. While you should start treating your Pug as an older dog at 7 years in regards to his health care, the exact point your dog starts acting like a senior Pug can be delayed—sometimes as late as their 10th or 15th year.

Signs of aging

The best way to know if your Pug is getting old is to look out for the signs:

- Graying fur on the muzzle
- Thinning coat
- Lower energy levels
- Stiff movements or hesitation to jump up on furniture
- Tooth loss or new bad breath
- Haziness in the eye lens
- Failing senses (smell, hearing, sight, etc.)
- Reduced tolerance for heat and cold
- New weight gain or weight loss
- Reduced appetite
- More frequent urination or new accidents in the house
- New snapping, snarling, or startle reactions

If you notice two or more of these signs of aging in your Pug, mention it at your next vet visit. They may recommend making some changes to your care routine.

Keeping an Aging Pug Comfortable

The biggest change you'll see as your Pug ages is in his ability to get around the house. The Pug's small stature means it takes a lot of effort to get up on human-sized furniture, and as his joints age, this gets more difficult. If you notice your Pug is struggling to get on the couch or bed, consider buying ramps or portable stairs. This will make it easier for your senior Pug to be with his humans.

A Pug's eyesight will often get less sharp as he ages. Some Pugs lose their sight entirely, especially those who had eye issues when they were younger. Eyesight isn't a dog's most important sense, and even a completely blind Pug can live a happy life, but you might want to make some adjustments to his living space if you notice your Pug is bumping into walls and furniture. Provide extra padding at corners and consider employing scent markers to help him navigate.

Finally, remember that your Pug will be more sensitive to both heat and cold when he's a senior. If your Pug normally lounges around on the floor, consider buying a few extra dog beds. You can also repurpose an old cardboard box by lining it with warm blankets. This will give your Pug comfortable, warm places to rest.

Best Dog Food for Senior Pugs

Since a Pug's activity level usually drops when he's older, obesity becomes more of a concern for senior Pugs. If you notice your Pug is starting to get chubby, you may want to reduce his daily intake to around 1/3 cup rather than 1/2 cup.

Alternatively, you could purchase senior dog food. These have fewer calories and less fat and can be the best dog food for senior Pugs since they often have a higher protein content. A dog's digestive tract becomes less efficient as he ages, making it harder to metabolize protein. A high-protein diet ensures your Pug's nutritional needs are still being met fully.

Some Pugs do go the other way, losing their appetite as they age. This often happens if the Pug loses his sense of smell. Warming up the food in the microwave can help release more odor and make it more appealing. If you normally feed your Pug dry food, consider a wet food instead, which has a stronger smell. You can mix it in with his dry food if you don't want to switch foods completely.

Health concerns

Once your Pug is over 7 years old, your vet will probably recommend coming in for check-ups more often—once every six months, as opposed to the annual visits common for healthy adult Pugs. This is so they can scan for signs of diseases associated with aging.

Control of both internal and external parasites is especially important in an older Pug. The immune system weakens with age, so these infestations will be more likely to cause secondary symptoms and infections. If your Pug goes outside a lot, make sure he's up-to-date on flea and tick treatments. Also, keep a close eye on his coat and contact the vet if you notice dry skin patches, bald spots, or other signs of mange.

The Pug's underbite makes dental health a concern as it ages. This is less likely to be a problem if you've followed a good dental hygiene routine throughout the Pug's life, but pay attention if your Pug's breath starts to smell bad, or if he seems to have difficulty chewing.

Many of the ailments associated with aging can come on quickly in Pugs. The good news is, your Pug will tell you he's struggling—as long as you know what to pay attention to. Be especially mindful of any changes in behavior. If your Pug suddenly snaps at you when you touch him, he may be in pain. Contact the vet if this happens consistently, and you may be able to get ahead of a more serious problem.

Your Trusted Pug Resource List

N ow that you know all about the Pug, you're probably wondering, "Where do I find Pugs for sale near me?" This Bonus Chapter is your answer! While it's certainly not a comprehensive list, it will get you started on your search for the perfect Pug.

Pug Clubs

- **Pug Dog Club of America (USA)**

  http://www.pugdogclubofamerica.com

  The official U.S. breed club recognized by the AKC. The PDCA is an excellent resource for locating breeders and rescue organizations, as well as general breed and care information. They also organize Pug shows and other breed events.

- **Pug Club of Canada**

  http://www.pugcanada.com/en-ca/home

  National breed club and affiliate with the Canadian Kennel Club (CKC). They offer resources on breeders and rescues, as well as organizing Pug Shows and other events throughout the nation.

- **Pug Dog Club (UK)**

  http://www.pugdogclub.org.uk

  The oldest Pug club in the world, the Pug Dog Club lists UK breeders as well as organizing breed competitions and Pug shows.

Pug Breeders in the United States

- **Andi Pugs**

  http://www.andipugs.com/

  New York

  One of only two Pug breeders to earn the AKC Silver level Breeders of Merit, their puppies excel at conformation and are bred with a commitment to health.

- **Azalea Kennels**

  https://www.azaleakennels.com/

  Alabama

  Small private home kennel breeding Pugs to conformation standard.

- **Bre-Z Manor Pugs**

  http://www.brezmanorpugs.com/

  Texas

  This breeder occasionally offers both puppies and adult Pugs. Their program emphasizes physical soundness and an outgoing personality.

- **Candyland Pugs**

  http://candylandpugs.homestead.com/

  Ohio

This small home breeder primarily breeds for the show ring, but occasionally has puppies available for sale. All puppies are bred for health and temperament, as well as the physical AKC standard.

- **Casull Pugs**

  http://casullpugs.com/

  New York

  Dedicated to Show and breeding-quality Pugs, the kennel owners take their dogs to rally, agility, and obedience competitions as well as the conformation ring.

- **Coral Bay Pugs & Papillons**

  http://www.coralbaypugs.com/

  Florida

  A 4-time winner of the PDCA's Breeder of the Year award, they have bred over 100 champion Pugs in their 30-plus year history as a kennel.

- **Double D's Pugs**

  http://www.doubledspugs.com/

  Ohio

  This selective breeding program has produced 31 champions, including 4 grand champions.

- **Harmony Pugs**

  http://www.harmonypugs.com/

  Texas

  A selective breeder that sells puppies both for the show ring and as home pets.

- **Heuberg Pugs**

  https://heubergpugs.com/

  Maryland

  With over 30 years of experience, they are a small kennel that breeds for quality over quantity.

- **Hill Country Pugs**

  http://hillcountrypugs.com.p11.hostingprod.com/ hillcountrypugs.html

  Texas

  Winner of the PDCA's Breeder of the Year award 3 times, their Pugs consistently place high in the conformation ring and have been the top Pug breeder in the nation for 6 consecutive years.

- **Honey Pugs**

  http://www.honeypugs.com/

  North Carolina

  This kennel typically raises two litters a year and is primarily concerned with the health and temperament of its puppies.

- **Jett Ranch (Millpond Pugs)**

  https://www.jettranch.com

  California

  A championship lineage is the basis of this AKC breeder of merit's success as a kennel.

- **Kelz Pugz**

  http://www.kelzpugz.com/

  New York

  Owned by a veterinarian who also handles and shows her animals, they have a well-established breeding program based on a championship bloodline.

- **Mountain Aire Pugs**

  http://mtnairepugs.com/

  Oregon

  Small home breeder dedicated to producing ideal family pets.

- **O-Day Pugs**

  https://www.odaypugs.com/

  Arizona

  AKC breeder of merit, known for both breeding and showing conformation winners.

- **Panini Pugs**

  https://www.breeders.net/detail.php?id=214688

  New Jersey

  Private breeder specializing in rare coat colors, including brindle, platinum, and white Pugs.

- **Pickwick Pugs**

  https://www.pickwickpugs.com/

  Alabama

  Hobby and show kennel with a selective breeding program. As obedience trainers as well as breeders, their Pugs have often worked on basic commands before being placed in a home.

- **Prima Pugs**

  https://www.primapugs.com/

  Oregon

  Selective breeders who emphasize a sound temperament and high health standards in their puppies.

- **Sapphire Bay Pugs**

  http://www.sapphirebaypugs.com/

  Pennsylvania

  This small-batch breeder is dedicated to maintaining the breed standard for conformation.

- **Snuggle Pugs**

  https://www.snugglepugs.com/

  Michigan

  Breeders of both show dogs and family pets, they breed with a focus on temperament and health.

- **Vanity Pugs**

  http://www.vanitypugs.com/

  Missouri

  This hobby kennel mainly breeds for showing. While they don't often have puppies available for sale, they are known for breeding to a high standard.

- **Wind Valley Pugs**

  http://www.windvalleypugs.com/

  Louisiana

  These breeders are equally known for showing their animals. They breed for individual health and the elevation of the Pug standard.

- **WindWalker Pugs**

  http://www.windwalkerpugs.com/

  Washington

  AKC Breeder of Merit, who are members of the Canadian Kennel Club, as well, showing their animals in both nation's competitions.

Pug Breeders in Canada

- **Cuddle Pugs**

  https://www.cuddlepugs.net/

  British Columbia

  Dedicated breeder committed to improving the health of their line

- **Devonsleigh Kennels**

  http://www.devonsleigh.com/

  Ontario

  Breeders of champions in both conformation and obedience, they put an emphasis on temperament and disposition in their puppies.

- **Gibby Pugs**

  https://www.gibbypugs.com/

  Alberta

  Offers both puppies for sale and a stud service for interested breeders.

- **Hyclass Pugs**

  https://hyclasspugs.com/index.html

  British Columbia

  Breeders of competition-quality Pugs, with both black Pugs and fawn Pugs available.

- **Pug Paws**

  http://www.pugpaws.com/

  Ontario

  Small breeder dedicated exclusively to breeding family pets, with all 4 common coat colors on offer.

- **Xoe Pugs**

  http://www.xoepugs.com/

  Alberta

  Championship breeders with 1-2 litters available for sale each year.

Pug Breeders in the U.K.

- **Kennel Club Assured Breeders**

  https://www.thekennelclub.org.uk/services/public/acbr/Default.aspx?breed=Pug

  A searchable database of Pug breeders, divided by county.

- **Conquell Pug Dogs**

  https://www.conquellpugs.co.uk/

  Kennel Club Assured Breeder that breeds for the show ring in both fawn and black coats.

- **Snugglepug**

  http://www.snugglepug.co.uk/

  Powys, Mid Wales

  Show kennel with both black and fawn Pugs available.

- **Tussilago Pugs**

  http://tussilagopugs.co.uk/

  Hampshire, England

  Assured breeders with the Kennel Club, they breed puppies ideal for the show ring, though they breed only occasionally.

Pug Rescue and Adoption in the United States

- **Colorado Pug Rescue**

  https://copugrescue.org/

  Colorado

  Volunteer rescue organization with a searchable list of Pugs available for adoption.

- **Dallas Fort Worth Pug Rescue**

  http://www.pugrescuenc.org/

  Texas

  Searchable site of Texas Pugs in need of new homes.

- **Delaware Valley Pug Rescue**

  https://www.dvpr.org/

  New Jersey

  Non-profit caring for Pugs in need throughout the Delaware Valley.

- **Mid-Michigan Pug Club**

  http://www.midmichiganpugclub.com/

  Michigan

  Affiliate of the PDCA that re-homes surrendered Pugs, regardless of age or medical conditions.

- **Midwest Pug Rescue**

  https://mnmidwestpugrescue.wildapricot.org/

  Minnesota

  This sanctuary for abandoned and stray Pugs organizes awareness events and offers training classes in addition to re-homing rescues.

- **Ohio Pug Rescue**

  http://www.ohiopugrescue.com/

  Ohio

  An all-volunteer organization that arranges foster care and permanent homes for abandoned Pugs.

- **Pug Rescue NC**

  http://www.pugrescuenc.org/

  North Carolina/Virginia

  A non-profit group dedicated to nursing injured Pugs back to health and finding them loving families.

- **Pug Rescue Network**

  http://pugrescuenetwork.com/pugrescuenetwork/homepage.html

  Midwest (Illinois, Indiana, Michigan, Ohio)

  Rescue and informational organization committed to the enduring health of the Pug breed.

- **Pug Rescue of New England**

  http://pugrescueofnewengland.org/

  Massachusetts (serves entire New England area)

  An organization that arranges Pug meetups and social events as well as helping homeless Pugs find families.

- **Pug Rescue of Sacramento**

  https://www.pugpros.org/

  California/Nevada

  An organization that takes in over 100 abandoned Pugs each year, providing medical care as well as helping them find loving homes.

- **Pug Rescue San Diego County**

  http://www.pugsandiego.com/index.php

  California

  An organization devoted to rescuing homeless pugs in southern California.

- **Seattle Pug Rescue**

  http://www.pugrescuenc.org/

  Washington

  This group organizes local Pug events in addition to its rescue efforts.

- **Yankee Pug Dog Club**

  http://www.yankeepugdogclub.org/about.asp

  Connecticut

  The New England chapter of the PDCA, they maintain a file of interested applicants for any Pugs in need of homes in the area.

Pug Rescue and Adoption in Canada

- **Manitoba Pug Rescue**

  https://www.manitobapugrescue.com/

  Manitoba

  Based in Winnipeg, this group fosters and re-homes abandoned Pugs.

- **Pugalug Pug Rescue**

  http://pugalug.com/

  Ontario

  Volunteer group committed to rescuing and re-homing Pugs.

- **Under My Wing Pug Rescue**

  https://www.undermywingpugrescue.com/

  Ontario

  Provides hospice care for ailing Pugs, along with providing fostering, surrender, and adoption services.

- **West Coast Canada Pug Rescue**

  http://www.westcoastcanadapugrescue.com/

  British Columbia

  Rescue group specifically serving British Columbia, with an emphasis on re-homing Pugs in the Vancouver area.

Pug Rescue and Adoption in the U.K.

- **Muffin Pug Rescue**

  https://www.muffinpugrescue.com/

  Non-profit devoted to rehabilitating and rehoming rescued Pugs.

- **The Pug Dog Welfare and Rescue Association**

  https://pugwelfare-rescue.org.uk/

  Volunteer rescue organization with fostering and adoption options.

- **Pug World**

  https://pugworld.co.uk/rescue.php

  An online resource for both Pug information and rescue opportunities.

www.ingramcontent.com/pod-product-compliance
Lightning Source LLC
Chambersburg PA
CBHW072011090426
42740CB00011B/2153